CONGRESSIONAL POLICIES, PRACTICES AND PROCEDURES

WAR POWERS RESOLUTION AFTER 34 YEARS AND THE CONTINUING POLITICAL DEBATE

JEREMIAH E. SANDERS
EDITOR

Nova Science Publishers, Inc.
New York

Copyright © 2010 by Nova Science Publishers, Inc.

All rights reserved. No part of this book may be reproduced, stored in a retrieval system or transmitted in any form or by any means: electronic, electrostatic, magnetic, tape, mechanical photocopying, recording or otherwise without the written permission of the Publisher.

For permission to use material from this book please contact us:
Telephone 631-231-7269; Fax 631-231-8175
Web Site: http://www.novapublishers.com

NOTICE TO THE READER

The Publisher has taken reasonable care in the preparation of this book, but makes no expressed or implied warranty of any kind and assumes no responsibility for any errors or omissions. No liability is assumed for incidental or consequential damages in connection with or arising out of information contained in this book. The Publisher shall not be liable for any special, consequential, or exemplary damages resulting, in whole or in part, from the readers' use of, or reliance upon, this material. Any parts of this book based on government reports are so indicated and copyright is claimed for those parts to the extent applicable to compilations of such works.

Independent verification should be sought for any data, advice or recommendations contained in this book. In addition, no responsibility is assumed by the publisher for any injury and/or damage to persons or property arising from any methods, products, instructions, ideas or otherwise contained in this publication.

This publication is designed to provide accurate and authoritative information with regard to the subject matter covered herein. It is sold with the clear understanding that the Publisher is not engaged in rendering legal or any other professional services. If legal or any other expert assistance is required, the services of a competent person should be sought. FROM A DECLARATION OF PARTICIPANTS JOINTLY ADOPTED BY A COMMITTEE OF THE AMERICAN BAR ASSOCIATION AND A COMMITTEE OF PUBLISHERS.

LIBRARY OF CONGRESS CATALOGING-IN-PUBLICATION DATA

War Powers Resolution after 34 years and the continuing political debate / editor, Jeremiah E. Sanders.
   p. cm.
Includes index.
ISBN 978-1-60692-787-8 (softcover)
1. United States. War Powers Resolution. 2. War and emergency powers--United States. 3. Legislative power--United States. 4. National security--United States. I. Sanders, Jeremiah E.
KF5060.W373 2009
342.73'062--dc22

2009041950

Published by Nova Science Publishers, Inc. † New York

CONTENTS

Preface		**ix**
Chapter 1	War Powers Resolution: Presidential Compliance *F. Richard Grimmett*	**1**
Chapter 2	The War Powers Resolution: After Thirty-Four Years *F. Richard Grimmett*	**27**
Chapter 3	War Powers Litigation Initiated by Members of Congress since the Enactment of the War Powers Resolution *M. David Ackerman*	**137**
Chapter Sources		**155**
Index		**157**

PREFACE

Two separate but closely related issues confront Congress each time the President introduces armed forces into a situation abroad that conceivably could lead to their involvement in hostilities. One issue concerns the division of war powers between the President and Congress, whether the use of armed forces falls within the purview of the congressional power to declare war and the War Powers Resolution (WPR). The other issue is whether or not Congress concurs in the wisdom of the action. This book does not deal with the substantive merits of using armed forces in specific cases, but rather with congressional authorization for military action, and the application and effectiveness of the WPR, as well as its application since enactment, providing detailed background on a variety of cases where it was utilized, or issues when its applicability were raised. In the post-Cold War world, Presidents have continued to commit U.S. Armed Forces into potential hostilities, sometimes without a specific authorization from Congress. Thus the War Powers Resolution and its purposes continues to be a potential subject of controversy.

This book consists of public documents which have been located, gathered, combined, reformatted, and enhanced with a subject index, selectively edited and bound to provide easy access.

Chapter 1- Two separate but closely related issues confront Congress each time the President introduces armed forces into a situation abroad that conceivably could lead to their involvement in hostilities. One issue concerns the division of war powers between the President and Congress, whether the use of armed forces falls within the purview of the congressional power to declare war and the War Powers Resolution (WPR). The other issue is whether or not Congress concurs in the wisdom of the action. This report does not deal with the substantive merits of using armed forces in specific cases, but rather with congressional authorization for military action, and the application and effectiveness of the WPR. The purpose of the WPR (P.L. 93-148, passed over President Nixon's veto on November 7, 1973) is to ensure that Congress and the President share in making decisions that may get the United States involved in hostilities. Compliance becomes an issue whenever the President introduces U.S. forces abroad in situations that might be construed as hostilities or imminent hostilities. Criteria for compliance include prior consultation with Congress, fulfillment of the reporting requirements, and congressional authorization. If the President has not complied fully, the issue becomes what action Congress should take to bring about compliance or to influence U.S. policy. A related issue has been congressional authorization of U.N. peacekeeping or other U.N.-sponsored actions.

For over three decades, war powers and the War Powers Resolution have been an issue in U.S. military actions in Asia, the Middle East, Africa, Central America, and Europe. Presidents have submitted 123 reports to Congress as a result of the War Powers Resolution, although only one (the Mayaguez situation) cited Section 4(a)(1) or specifically stated that forces had been introduced into hostilities or imminent hostilities. Congress invoked the WPR in the Multinational Force in Lebanon Resolution (P.L. 98-119), which authorized the Marines to remain in Lebanon for 18 months. In addition, P.L. 102-1, enacted in January 1991, authorizing the use of U.S. armed forces in response to Iraqi aggression against Kuwait, stated that it constituted specific statutory authorization within the meaning of the WPR. On November 9, 1993, the House used a section of the WPR to state that U.S. forces should be withdrawn from Somalia by March 31, 1994; Congress had already taken this action in appropriations legislation. War powers have been at issue in former Yugoslavia/Bosnia/Kosovo, Iraq, and Haiti. Authorizing military actions in response to the terrorist attacks against the United States of September 11, 2001, through P.L. 107-40 directly involved war powers. The continued use of force to obtain Iraqi compliance with U.N. resolutions remained a war powers issue from the end of the Gulf war on February 28, 1991, until the enactment of P.L. 107-243, in October 2002, which explicitly authorized the President to use force against Iraq, an authority he exercised in March 2003, and continues to exercise for military operations in Iraq.

Debate continues on whether using the War Powers Resolution is effective as a means of assuring congressional participation in decisions that might get the United States involved in a significant military conflict. Proposals have been made to modify or repeal the resolution. None have been enacted to date. This report will be updated as events warrant.

Preface

xi

Chapter 2 - This report discusses and assesses the War Powers Resolution, its application since enactment in 1973, providing detailed background on a variety of cases where it was utilized, or issues of its applicability were raised. It will be revised biannually.

In the post-Cold War world, Presidents have continued to commit U.S. Armed Forces into potential hostilities, sometimes without a specific authorization from Congress. Thus the War Powers Resolution and its purposes continues to be a potential subject of controversy. On June 7, 1995 the House defeated, by a vote of 217-201, an amendment to repeal the central features of the War Powers Resolution that have been deemed unconstitutional byeveryPresident since the law's enactment in 1973. In 1999, after the President committed U.S. military forces to action in Yugoslavia without congressional authorization, Representative Tom Campbell used expedited procedures under the Resolution to force a debate and votes on U.S. military action in Yugoslavia, and later sought, unsuccessfully, through a federal court suit to enforce Presidential compliance with the terms of the War Powers Resolution.

The War Powers Resolution (P.L. 93-148) was passed over the veto of President Nixon on November 7, 1973, to provide procedures for Congress and the President to participate in decisions to send U.S. Armed Forces into hostilities. Section 4(a)(1) requires the President to report to Congress any introduction of U.S. forces into hostilities or imminent hostilities. When such a report is submitted, or is required to be submitted, section 5(b) requires that the use of forces must be terminated within 60 to 90 days unless Congress authorizes such use or extends the time period. Section 3 requires that the "President in every possible instance shall consult with Congress before introducing" U.S. Armed Forces into hostilities or imminent hostilities.

From 1975 through 2007, Presidents have submitted 123 reports as the result of the War Powers Resolution, but only one, the 1975 *Mayaguez* seizure, cited section 4(a)(1) which triggers the time limit, and in this case the military action was completed and U.S. armed forces had disengaged from the area of conflict when the report was made. The reports submitted by the President since enactment of the War Powers Resolution cover a range of military activities from embassy evacuations to full scale combat military operations, such as the Persian Gulf conflict, and the 2003 war with Iraq, the intervention in Kosovo and the anti-terrorism actions in Afghanistan. In some instances U.S. Armed Forces have been used in hostile situations without formal reports to Congress under the War Powers Resolution. On one occasion, Congress exercised its authority to determine that the requirements of section 4(a)(1) became operative on August 29, 1983, through passage of the Multinational Force in Lebanon Resolution (P.L. 98-

119). In 1991 and 2002, Congress authorized, by law, the use of military force against Iraq. In several instances neither the President, Congress, nor the courts have been willing to trigger the War Powers Resolution mechanism.

Chapter 3 - Article I, § 8, of the Constitution confers on Congress the power to "declare War." Modern Presidents, however, have contended that, notwithstanding this clause, they do not need Congressional authorization to use force. Partly in response to that contention, and because of widespread concern that Congress had allowed its war power to atrophy in the Korean and Vietnam conflicts, Congress in 1973 enacted the War Powers Resolution (WPR). The WPR, *inter cilia,* requires the President to report to Congress any time U.S. military forces are introduced into "hostilities or ... situations where imminent involvement in hostilities is clearly indicated by the circumstances." Once such a report is submitted, the WPR requires that the forces must be withdrawn within 60 days (90 days in specified circumstances) unless Congress declares war or otherwise authorizes their continued involvement.

Nonetheless, subsequent Presidents have continued to maintain that they have sufficient authority independent of Congress to initiate the use of military force; and all Presidents from Nixon to Bush have viewed the WPR as trenching on their constitutional powers. Congress has on four occasions enacted authorizations specifically waiving the 60-90 day limitation on the use of force otherwise imposed by the WPR. But in six other instances involving U.S. military involvement in El Salvador, Nicaragua, Grenada, the Persian Gulf conflict between Iraq and Iran, Iraq's invasion of Kuwait (prior to the Congressional authorization), and NATO's action in Kosovo, Presidential avoidance and Congressional inaction have led a number of Members to initiate suits in federal court to compel various Presidents to comply with the reporting and/or troop withdrawal requirements of the Resolution or to otherwise recognize Congress' war powers. A seventh suit, recently decided, sought to enjoin the President from using military force against Iraq on the grounds such an action would exceed the authority conferred by Congress in the statute it adopted in October, 2002.

In every instance to date (with the exception of part of the last decision) the courts have found reasons not to render a decision on the merits of the suits. The courts have variously found the political question doctrine, the equitable/remedial discretion doctrine, the issue of ripeness, and the question of Congressional standing to preclude judicial resolution of the matter. Although not ruling out the possibility that a conflict over the use of force between Congress and the President could require a judicial resolution, the courts so far have deemed the matter to be one for the political branches to resolve.

This report summarizes the seven cases initiated by Members of Congress. It will be updated as circumstances warrant.

In: War Powers Resolution after 34 Years...   ISBN: 978-1-60692-787-8
Editors: Jeremiah E. Sanders   © 2010 Nova Science Publishers, Inc.

Chapter 1

WAR POWERS RESOLUTION: PRESIDENTIAL COMPLIANCE

F. Richard Grimmett
International Security Foreign Affairs, Defense, and Trade Division

SUMMARY

Two separate but closely related issues confront Congress each time the President introduces armed forces into a situation abroad that conceivably could lead to their involvement in hostilities. One issue concerns the division of war powers between the President and Congress, whether the use of armed forces falls within the purview of the congressional power to declare war and the War Powers Resolution (WPR). The other issue is whether or not Congress concurs in the wisdom of the action. This report does not deal with the substantive merits of using armed forces in specific cases, but rather with congressional authorization for military action, and the application and effectiveness of the WPR. The purpose of the WPR (P.L. 93-148, passed over President Nixon's veto on November 7, 1973) is to ensure that Congress and the President share in making decisions that may get the United States involved in hostilities. Compliance becomes an issue whenever the President introduces U.S. forces abroad in situations that might be construed as hostilities or imminent hostilities. Criteria for compliance include prior consultation with Congress, fulfillment of the reporting requirements, and congressional authorization. If the President has not complied fully, the issue becomes what action Congress should take to bring about compliance or to influence U.S. policy. A related issue has been congressional authorization of U.N. peacekeeping or other U.N.-sponsored actions.

For over three decades, war powers and the War Powers Resolution have been an issue in U.S. military actions in Asia, the Middle East, Africa, Central America, and Europe. Presidents have submitted 123 reports to Congress as a result of the War Powers Resolution, although only one (the Mayaguez situation) cited Section 4(a)(1) or specifically stated that forces had been introduced into hostilities or imminent hostilities. Congress invoked the WPR in the Multinational Force in Lebanon Resolution (P.L. 98-119), which authorized the Marines to remain in Lebanon for 18 months. In addition, P.L. 102-1, enacted in January 1991, authorizing the use of U.S. armed forces in response to Iraqi aggression against Kuwait, stated that it constituted specific statutory authorization within the meaning of the WPR. On November 9, 1993, the House used a section of the WPR to state that U.S. forces should be withdrawn from Somalia by March 31, 1994; Congress had already taken this action in appropriations legislation. War powers have been at issue in former Yugoslavia/Bosnia/Kosovo, Iraq, and Haiti. Authorizing military actions in response to the terrorist attacks against the United States of September 11, 2001, through P.L. 107-40 directly involved war powers. The continued use of force to obtain Iraqi compliance with U.N. resolutions remained a war powers issue from the end of the Gulf war on February 28, 1991, until the enactment of P.L. 107-243, in October 2002, which explicitly authorized the President to use force against Iraq, an authority he exercised in March 2003, and continues to exercise for military operations in Iraq.

Debate continues on whether using the War Powers Resolution is effective as a means of assuring congressional participation in decisions that might get the United States involved in a significant military conflict. Proposals have been made to modify or repeal the resolution. None have been enacted to date. This report will be updated as events warrant.

MOST RECENT DEVELOPMENTS

On December 14, 2007, the President sent to Congress "**consistent** with the War Powers Resolution," **a consolidated report giving details** of ongoing

United States military deployments and operations "in support of the war on terror,"and in support of the NATO-led Kosovo Force (KFOR). The President reported that various U.S. "combat-equipped and combat-support forces" were deployed to "a number of locations in the Central, Pacific, European, and Southern Command areas of operation" and were engaged in combat operations against al-Qaida terrorists and their supporters. The United States is currently "pursuing and engaging remnant alQaida and Taliban fighters in Afghanistan." U.S. forces in Afghanistan currently total approximately 25,900. Of this total, "approximately 15,180 are assigned to the International Security Assistance Force (ISAF) in Afghanistan." The U.S. military continues to support peacekeeping operations in Kosovo, specifically, the NATO-led Kosovo Force (KFOR). Currently, the U.S. contribution to KFOR in Kosovo is approximately 1,498 military personnel.

BACKGROUND AND ANALYSIS

Under the Constitution, war powers are divided. Congress has the power to declare war and raise and support the armed forces (Article I, Section 8), while the President is Commander in Chief (Article II, Section 2). It is generally agreed that the Commander in Chief role gives the President power to repel attacks against the United States and makes him responsible for leading the armed forces. During the Korean and Vietnam wars, the United States found itself involved for many years in undeclared wars. Many Members of Congress became concerned with the erosion of congressional authority to decide when the United States should become involved in a war or the use of armed forces that might lead to war. On November 7, 1973, Congress passed the War Powers Resolution (P.L. 93-148) over the veto of President Nixon.

The War Powers Resolution (WPR) states that the President's powers as Commander in Chief to introduce U.S. forces into hostilities or imminent hostilities are exercised only pursuant to (1) a declaration of war; (2) specific statutory authorization; or (3) a national emergency created by an attack on the United States or its forces. It requires the President in every possible instance to consult with Congress before introducing American armed forces into hostilities or imminent hostilities unless there has been a declaration of war or other specific congressional authorization. It also requires the President to report to Congress any introduction of forces into hostilities or imminent hostilities, Section 4(a)(1); into foreign territory while equipped for combat, Section 4(a)(2); or in numbers which substantially enlarge U.S. forces equipped for combat already in a foreign nation, Section 4(a)(3). Once a report is submitted "or required to be submitted" under Section 4(a)(1), Congress must authorize the use of forces within 60 to 90 days or the forces must be withdrawn. (For detailed background, see CRS Report RL3 2267, *The War Powers Resolution: After Thirty-Three Years,* by Richard F. Grimmett, and CRS Report RL3 1133, *Declarations of War and Authorizations for the Use of Military Force: Historical Background and Legal Implications,* by Jennifer Elsea and Richard F. Grimmett.) It is important to note that since the War Powers Resolution's enactment, over President Nixon's veto in 1973, every President has taken the position that it is an unconstitutional infringement by the Congress on the President's authority as Commander in Chief. The courts have not directly addressed this question.

UNITED NATIONS ACTIONS

U.N. Security Council resolutions provide authority for U.S. action under international law. Whether congressional authorization is required under domestic law depends on the types of U.N. action and is governed by the Constitution, the U.N. Participation Act (P.L. 79-264, as amended), as well as by the War Powers Resolution. Section 8(b) of the War Powers Resolution exempts only participation in headquarters operations of joint military commands established prior to 1973.

For armed actions under Articles 42 and 43 of the U.N. Charter, Section 6 of the U.N. Participation Act authorizes the President to negotiate special agreements with the Security Council, subject to the approval of Congress, providing for the numbers and types of armed forces and facilities to be made available to the Security Council. Once the agreements have been concluded, further congressional authorization is not necessary, but no such agreements have been concluded. Some Members have sought to encourage negotiation of military agreements under Article 43 of the U.N. Charter. Questions include whether congressional approval is required only for an initial agreement on providing peacekeeping forces in general, or for each agreement to provide forces in specific situations, and how such approvals would relate to the War Powers Resolution.

Section 7 of the U.N. Participation Act authorizes the detail of up to 1,000 personnel to serve in any noncombatant capacity for certain U.N. peaceful settlement activities. The United States has provided personnel to several U.N. peacekeeping missions, such as observers to the U.N. Truce Supervision Organization in Palestine. In these instances, controversy over the need for congressional authorization has not occurred because the action appeared to fall within the authorization in Section 7 of the Participation Act. Controversy has arisen when forces have been deployed in larger numbers or as possible combatants.

In the 103rd Congress, Members used several vehicles in seeking some control over future peacekeeping actions wherever they might occur. Both the Defense Appropriations Act for FY1 994, P.L. 103-139 (Section 8153), and for FY1 995, P.L. 103- 335 (Section 8103), stated the sense of Congress that funds should not be used for U.N. peacekeeping or peace enforcement operations unless the President consulted with Congress at least 15 days in advance whenever possible. Section 1502 of the Defense Authorization for FY1994, P.L. 103-60, required the President to submit by April 1, 1994, a report on multinational peacekeeping including the requirement of congressional approval for participation and the applicability of the War Powers Resolution and the U.N. Participation Act.

Along similar lines, the conference report accompanying the Department of State Appropriations Act for FY1994, H.R. 2519 (P.L. 103-121, signed October 27, 1993), called for the Secretary of State to notify both Appropriations Committees 15 days in advance, where practicable, of a vote by the U.N. Security Council to establish any new or expanded peacekeeping mission. The Foreign Relations Authorization Act, P.L. 103-236, signed April 30, 1994, established new requirements for consultation with Congress on U.S. Participation in U.N. Peacekeeping Operations. Section 407 required monthly consultations on the status of peacekeeping operations and advance reports on resolutions that would authorize a new U.N. peacekeeping operation. It also required 15 days' advance notice of any U.S. assistance to support U.N. peacekeeping operations and a quarterly report on all assistance that had been provided to the U.N. for peacekeeping operations. To permit presidential flexibility, conferees explained, the quarterly report need not include temporary duty assignments of U.S. personnel in support of peacekeeping operations of less than 20 personnel in any one case.

The following discussion provides background on major cases of U.S. military involvement in overseas operations in recent years that have raised War Powers questions.

Former Yugoslavia/Bosnia

The issue of war powers and whether congressional authorization is necessary for U.S. participation in U.N. action was also raised by efforts to halt fighting in the former territory of Yugoslavia, particularly in Bosnia. The United States participated without congressional authorization in airlifts into Sarajevo, naval monitoring of sanctions, aerial enforcement of a "no-fly zone," and aerial enforcement of safe havens.

Because some of the U.S. action has been taken within a NATO framework, action in Bosnia has raised the broader issue of whether action under NATO is exempt from the requirements of the War Powers Resolution or its standard for the exercise of war powers under the Constitution. Article 11 of the North Atlantic Treaty states that its provisions are to be carried out by the parties "in accordance with their respective constitutional processes," implying some role for Congress in the event of war. Section 8(a) of the War Powers Resolution states that authority to introduce U.S. forces into hostilities is not to be inferred from any treaty, ratified before or after 1973, unless implementing legislation specifically authorizes such introduction and says it is intended to constitute an authorization within the meaning of the War Powers Resolution. Section 8(b) states that nothing in the Resolution should be construed to require further authorization for U.S. participation in the headquarters operations of military commands established before 1973, such as NATO headquarters operations.

On August 13, 1992, the U.N. Security Council adopted Resolution 770 calling on all nations to take "all measures necessary" to facilitate the delivery of humanitarian assistance to Sarajevo. On August 11, 1992, the Senate passed S.Res. 330 urging the President to work for such a resolution and pledging funds for participation, but saying that no U.S. military personnel should be introduced into hostilities without clearly defined objectives. On the same day, the House passed H.Res. 554 urging the Security Council to authorize measures, including the use of force, to ensure humanitarian relief. Thus, both chambers of Congress supported action but not by legislation authorizing the use of U.S. forces. For details of congressional actions relating to Bosnia from 1993 through 1995, see CRS Report RL32267, *The War Powers Resolution: After Thirty-Three Years*, by Richard F. Grimmett.

In late 1995, the issue of war powers and Bosnia was raised again as President Clinton sent more than 20,000 American combat troops to Bosnia as part of a NATO-led peacekeeping force. In December 1995, Congress considered and voted on a number of bills and resolutions, but the House and

War Powers Resolution: Presidential Compliance

Senate could not come to consensus on any single measure. Subsequently, President Clinton in December 1996, agreed to provide up to 8,500 ground troops to participate in a NATO-led follow-on force in Bosnia termed the Stabilization Force (SFOR). On March 18, 1998, the House defeated by a vote of 193-225, H.Con.Res. 227, a resolution directing the President, pursuant to section 5(c) of the War Powers Resolution to remove United States Armed Forces from the Republic of Bosnia and Herzegovina (H.Rept. 105-442). (For additional information, see CRS Report RL32392, *Bosnia and Herzegovina: Issues for U.S. Policy*, by Steven Woehrel, CRS Report RL32282, *Bosnia and Kosovo: U.S. Military Operations*, by Steve Bowman, and CRS Report RL32267, *The War Powers Resolution: After Thirty-Three Years*, by Richard F. Grimmett.)

Kosovo

The issue of presidential authority to deploy forces in the absence of congressional authorization, under the War Powers Resolution, or otherwise, became an issue of significant controversy in late March 1999 when President Clinton ordered U.S. military forces to participate in a NATO-led military operation in Kosovo. This action has become the focus of an ongoing policy debate over the purpose and scope of U.S. military involvement in Kosovo. The President's action to commit forces to the NATO Kosovo operation also led to a suit in Federal District Court for the District of Columbia by some Members of Congress seeking a judicial finding that the President was violating the War Powers Resolution and the Constitution by using military forces in Yugoslavia in the absence of authorization from the Congress.

The Kosovo controversy began in earnest when on March 26, 1999, President Clinton notified the congress "consistent with the War Powers Resolution", that on March 24, 1999, U.S. military forces, at his direction and in coalition with NATO allies, had commenced air strikes against Yugoslavia in response to the Yugoslav government's campaign of violence and repression against the ethnic Albanian population in Kosovo. Prior to the President's action, the Senate, on March 23, 1999, had passed, by a vote of 58-41, S.Con.Res. 21, a nonbinding resolution expressing the sense of the Congress that the President was authorized to conduct "military air operations and missile strikes in cooperation with our NATO allies against the Federal Republic of Yugoslavia (Serbia and Montenegro)."

Subsequently, the House voted on a number of measures relating to U.S. participation in the NATO operation in Kosovo. On April 28, 1999, the House of Representatives passed H.R. 1569, by a vote of 249-180. This bill would prohibit the use of funds appropriated to the Defense Department from being used for the deployment of "ground elements" of the U.S. Armed Forces in the Federal Republic of Yugoslavia unless that deployment is specifically authorized by law. On that same day the House defeated H.Con.Res. 82, by a vote of 139-290. This resolution would have directed the President, pursuant to section 5(c) of the War Powers Resolution, to remove U.S. Armed Forces from their positions in connection with the present operations against the Federal Republic of Yugoslavia. On April 28, 1999, the House also defeated H.J.Res. 44, by a vote of 2-427. This joint resolution would have declared a state of war between the United States and the "Government of the Federal Republic of Yugoslavia." The House on that same day also defeated, on a 213-213 tie vote, S.Con.Res. 21, the Senate resolution passed on March 23, 1999, that supported military air operations and missile strikes against Yugoslavia. On April 30, 1999, Representative Tom Campbell and 17 other members of the House filed suit in Federal District Court for the District of Columbia seeking a ruling requiring the President to obtain authorization from Congress before continuing the air war, or taking other military action against Yugoslavia.

The Senate, on May 4, 1999, by a vote of 78-22, tabled S.J.Res. 20, a joint resolution, sponsored by Senator John McCain, that would authorize the President "to use all necessary force and other means, in concert with United States allies, to accomplish United States and North Atlantic Treaty Organization objectives in the Federal Republic of Yugoslavia (Serbia and Montenegro)." The House, meanwhile, on May 6, 1999, by a vote of 117-301, defeated an amendment by Representative Istook to H.R. 1664, the FY1999 defense supplemental appropriations bill, that would have prohibited the expenditure of funds in the bill to implement any plan to use U.S. ground forces to invade Yugoslavia, except in time of war. Congress, meanwhile, on May 20, 1999, cleared for the President's signature, H.R. 1141, an emergency supplemental appropriations bill for FY1999, that provided billions in funding for the existing U.S. Kosovo operation.

On May 25, 1999, the 60th day had passed since the President notified Congress of his actions regarding U.S. participation in military operations in Kosovo. Representative Campbell, and those who joined his suit, noted to the Federal Court that this was a clear violation of the language of the War Powers Resolution stipulating a withdrawal of U.S. forces from the area of hostilities occur after 60 days in the absence of congressional authorization to continue, or a presidential request to Congress for an extra 30 day period to safely withdraw. The President did not seek such a 30-day extension, noting instead that the War Powers Resolution is constitutionally defective. On June 8, 1999, Federal District Judge Paul L. Friedman dismissed the suit of Representative Campbell and others that sought to have the court rule that President Clinton was in violation of the War Powers Resolution and the Constitution by conducting military activities in Yugoslavia without having received prior authorization from Congress. The judge ruled that Representative Campbell and others lacked legal standing to bring the suit (*Campbell v. Clinton*, 52 F. Supp. 2d 34 (D.D.C. 1999)). Representative Campbell appealed the ruling on June 24, 1999, to the U.S. Court of Appeals for the District of Columbia. The appeals court agreed to hear the case. On February 18, 2000, the appeals court affirmed the opinion of the District Court that Representative Campbell and his co-plaintiffs lacked standing to sue the President. (Campbell v. Clinton, 203 F.3d 19 (D.C. Cir. 2000). On May 18, 2000, Representative Campbell and 30 other Members of Congress appealed this decision to the United States Supreme Court. On October 2, 2000, the United States Supreme Court, without comment, refused to hear the appeal of Representative Campbell thereby letting stand the holding of the U.S. Court of Appeals. (Campbell v. Clinton, *cert. denied*, 531U.S. 815 October 2, 2000). On May 18, 2000, the Senate defeated by, a vote of 47-53, an amendment to S. 2521, the **Senate's** version of the Military Construction Appropriations Act, FY2001, that would have, among other things, terminated funding for the continued deployment of U.S. ground combat troops in Kosovo after July 1, 2001 unless the President sought and received Congressional authorization to keep U.S. troops in Kosovo. (For detailed discussion of major issues see CRS Report RL3 1053, *Kosovo and U.S. Policy*, by Steven J. Woehrel and Julie Kim; CRS Report RL30352, *War Powers Litigation Initiated by Members of Congress Since the Enactment of the War Powers Resolution*, by David M. Ackerman.)

Iraq: Post 1991

During the week of October 3, 1994, Iraq began sending two additional divisions to join regular forces in southern Iraq, close to the border of Kuwait. On October 8, President Clinton responded by sending about 30,000 additional U.S. forces and additional combat planes to join the forces already in the Gulf area. He said the United States would honor its commitment to defend Kuwait and enforce U.N. resolutions on Iraq. Congress recessed on October 8 until November 29, 1994, so it did not discuss the issue of congressional authorization. On October 28, President Clinton reported to Congress that by October 15 there were clear indications that Iraq had redeployed its forces to their original location. On November 7, the Defense Department announced 7,000 of the U.S. forces would be withdrawn before Christmas.

Earlier, three continuing situations in Iraq since the end of Desert Storm brought about the use of U.S. forces and thus raised war powers issues. The first situation resulted from the Iraqi government's repression of Kurdish and Shiite groups. U.N. Security Council Resolution 688 of April 5, 1991, condemned the repression of the Iraqi civilian population and appealed for contributions to humanitarian relief efforts. The second situation stemmed from the U.N. cease-fire resolution of April 3, 1991, Security Council Resolution 687, which called for Iraq to accept the destruction or removal of chemical and biological weapons, and international control of its nuclear materials.

The third situation was related to both of the earlier ones. On August 26, 1992, the United States, Britain, and France began a "no-fly" zone, banning Iraqi fixed wing and helicopter flights south of the 32nd parallel and creating a limited security zone in the south, where Shiite groups are concentrated. After violations of the no-fly zones and various other actions by Iraq, on January 13, 1993, the outgoing Bush Administration announced that aircraft from the United States and coalition partners had attacked missile bases in southern Iraq and that the United States was deploying a battalion task force to Kuwait to underline the U.S. continuing commitment to Kuwait's independence. On January 6, 1993, the United States gave Iraq an ultimatum to remove newly deployed missiles in the no-fly zone. On January 19, 1993, President George H.W. Bush reported to Congress that U.S. aircraft on December 27, 1992, had shot down an Iraqi aircraft that had entered the no-fly zone and had undertaken further military actions on January 13, 17, and 18.

President Clinton said on January 21, 1993, that the United States would adhere to the policy toward Iraq set by the former Bush Administration, and on January 22, 23, April 9 and 18, June 19, and August 19, 1993, U.S. aircraft fired at targets in Iraq after pilots detected Iraqi radar or anti-aircraft fire directed at them. A number of such incidents occurred while planes patrolled the no-fly zone. On June 6, 1994, President Clinton reported that over the previous two years, the northern no-fly zone had deterred Iraq from a military offensive in the northern zone. Iraqi forces had responded to the no-fly zone in the south, he reported, by continuing to use land-based artillery to shell marsh villages. In addition, Iraq was conducting a large search and destroy operation and razing and burning marsh villages, in violation of U.N. Security Council Resolution 688. Until Iraq fully complied with all relevant U.N. Security Council resolutions, he reported, the United States would maintain sanctions and other measures designed to achieve compliance.

A war powers issue for years was whether the use of U.S. force in Iraq in the period after the early 1991 Desert Storm conflict had been authorized by Congress. P.L. 102-1 authorized the President to use U.S. armed forces pursuant to U.N. Security Council Resolution 678 to achieve implementation of previous Security Council Resolutions; Security Council Resolution 687 was adopted after this. On August 2, 1991, the Senate adopted an amendment to the Defense Authorization bill for FY1992 supporting the use of all necessary means to achieve the goals of Resolution 687. Senator Dole said the amendment was not intended to authorize the use of force by the President, and that in his view in the current circumstances the President required no specific authorization from Congress. As enacted, Section 1095 of P.L. 102-190 states the sense of Congress that it supports the use of all necessary means to achieve the goals of Security Council Resolution 687 as being consistent with the Authorization for Use of Military Force Against Iraq Resolution. The bill (Section 1096) also included an amendment by Senator Pell supporting the use of all necessary means to protect Iraq's Kurdish minority, consistent with relevant U.N. resolutions and authorities contained in P.L. 102-1.

In addition to these continuing situations, on June 28, 1993, president Clinton reported to Congress that on June 26, U. S. naval forces had launched a Tomahawk cruise missile strike on the Iraqi Intelligence Service's main command and control complex in Baghdad and that the military action was completed. He said the Iraqi Intelligence Service had planned the failed attempt to assassinate former President Bush during his visit to Kuwait in April 1993. On September 5, 1996, President Clinton reported to Congress on U.S. military actions in Iraq to obtain compliance with U.N. Security Council Resolutions, especially in light of attacks by Iraqi military forces against the Kurdish-controlled city of Irbil. U.S. actions ordered by the President included extending the no-fly zone in southern Iraq from 32 to 33 degrees north latitude, and cruise missile attacks from B-52H bombers and ships in the USS Carl Vinson Battle Group against fixed, surface-to-air missile sites, command and control centers, and air defense control facilities south of the 33rd parallel in Iraq. Except for the report of June 28, 1993, Presidents Bush and Clinton did not cite the War Powers Resolution in their reports related to military activities in Iraq in the period after the 1991 Gulf War. Rather, they submitted them "consistent with" P.L. 102-1, which required the President to submit a report to the Congress at least once every 60 days on the status of efforts to obtain compliance by Iraq with the U.N. Security Council resolution adopted in response to the Iraq aggression.

Starting in 1998 and through the end of the Clinton Administration, Iraq's refusal to permit U.N. weapons inspection teams access to various Iraqi sites, and Iraqi threats to U.S. aircraft policing the "no-fly zones" resulted in U.S. military action on numerous occasions against Iraqi military forces and targets in the "no-fly zones." President Clinton chose to report these actions under the requirements of P.L. 102-1, rather than the War Powers Resolution. In early February 2001, President George W. Bush authorized U.S. aircraft to attack Iraqi radar installations in Southern Iraq believed to threaten allied forces enforcing the "no-fly zone." Additional bombings of Iraqi sites were authorized and took place from the summer of 2001 into March 2003. Such actions, in the past, were reported under P.L. 102-1. Congress provided authorization for future military action, under specified conditions, through passage of P.L. 107-243 signed into law on October 16, 2002. In a report to Congress on January 20, 2003, pursuant to P.L. 107-243, President Bush stated that information required to be reported regarding actions taken against Iraq required by section 3 of P.L. 102-1 would in the future be included in the reports required by P.L. 107-243. On March 19, 2003, President Bush directed U.S. Armed Forces to commence combat operations against Iraq to enforce its disarmament. Since he announced the end of major combat operations against Iraq on May 1, 2003, the President has made periodic reports on the current situation in Iraq "consistent with" P.L. 107-243, which have become the equivalent of reports to Congress envisioned by the War Powers Resolution. For a recent example of these reports to Congress see House Document 108-231, 108th Congress, 2nd session, submitted November 4, 2004. (For related information, see CRS Report RL3 1701, *Iraq: U.S. Military Operations*, by Steve Bowman, and CRS Report RL31339, *Iraq: U.S. Regime Change Efforts and Post-Saddam Governance*, by Kenneth Katzman.)

Haiti

On July 3, 1993, Haitian military leader Raoul Cedras and deposed President Jean-Bertrand Aristide signed an agreement at Governors Island providing for the restoration of President Aristide on October 30. The United Nations and Organization of American States took responsibility for verifying compliance. Because the Haitian authorities did not comply with the agreement, on October 13, 1993, the U.N. Security Council voted to restore sanctions against Haiti. On October 20, President Clinton submitted a report "consistent with the War Powers Resolution" that U.S. ships had begun to enforce a U.N. embargo. Some Members of Congress complained that Congress had not been consulted about nor authorized the action. On October 18, 1993, Senator Dole said he would offer an amendment to the FY1 994 Defense Appropriations bill (H.R. 3116) which would require congressional authorization for all deployments into Haitian waters and airspace unless the President made specified certifications. Congressional leaders and Administration officials negotiated the terms of the amendment. As enacted, Section 8147 of P.L. 103-139 stated the sense that funds should not be obligated or expended for U.S. military operations in Haiti unless the operations were (1) authorized in advance by Congress, (2) necessary to protect or evacuate U.S. citizens, (3) vital to the national security and there was not sufficient time to receive congressional authorization, or (4) the President submitted a report in advance that the intended deployment met certain criteria.

On May 6, 1994, the U.N. Security Council adopted Resolution 917 calling for measures to tighten the embargo. On June 10, 1994, President Clinton announced steps being taken to intensify the pressure on Haiti's military leaders that included assisting the Dominican Republic to seal its border with Haiti, using U.S. naval patrol boats to detain ships suspected of violating the sanctions, a ban on commercial air traffic, and sanctions on financial transactions. As conditions in Haiti worsened, President Clinton stated he would not rule out the use of force, and gradually the use of force appeared certain. Many Members continued to contend congressional authorization was necessary for any invasion of Haiti. On July 31, the U.N. Security Council authorized a multinational force to use "all necessary means to facilitate the departure from Haiti of the military leadership ... on the understanding that the cost of implementing this temporary operation will be borne by the participating Member States" (Resolution 940, 1994).

On August 3, the Senate adopted an amendment to the Department of Veterans Affairs appropriation, H.R. 4624, by a vote of 100-0 expressing its sense that the Security Council Resolution did not constitute authorization for the deployment of U.S. forces in Haiti under the Constitution or the War Powers Resolution, but the amendment was not agreed to in conference. President Clinton said the same day that he would welcome the support of Congress but did not agree that he was constitutionally mandated to obtain it.

14   F. Richard Grimmett

On September 15, 1994, in an address to the Nation, President Clinton said he had called up the military reserve and ordered two aircraft carriers into the region. His message to the military dictators was to leave now or the United States would force them from power. The first phase of military action would remove the dictators from power and restore Haiti's democratically elected government. The second phase would involve a much smaller force joining with forces from other U.N. members which would leave Haiti after 1995 elections were held and a new government installed.

While the Defense Department continued to prepare for an invasion within days, on September 16 President Clinton sent to Haiti a negotiating team of former President Jimmy Carter, former Joint Chiefs of Staff Chairman Colin Powell, and Senate Armed Services Committee Chairman Sam Nunn. Again addressing the Nation on September 18, President Clinton announced that the military leaders had agreed to step down by October 15, and agreed to the immediate introduction of troops from the 15,000 member international coalition beginning September 19. He said the agreement was only possible because of the credible and imminent threat of multinational force. He emphasized the mission still had risks and there remained possibilities of violence directed at U.S. troops, but the agreement minimized those risks. He also said that under U.N. Security Council resolution 940, a 25-nation international coalition would soon go to Haiti to begin the task of restoring democratic government. Also on September 18, President Clinton reported to Congress on the objectives in accordance with the sense expressed in Section 8147 (c) of P.L. 103-139, the FY1994 Defense Appropriations Act.

U.S. forces entered Haiti on September 19, 1994. On September 21, President Clinton reported "consistent with the War Powers Resolution" the deployment of 1,500 troops, to be increased by several thousand. (At the peak in September there were about 21,000 U.S. forces in Haiti.) He said the U.S. presence would not be open-ended but would be replaced after a period of months by a U.N. peacekeeping force, although some U.S. forces would participate in and be present for the duration of the U.N. mission. The forces were involved in the first hostilities on September 24 when U.S. Marines killed 10 armed Haitian resisters in a fire-fight.

On October 3, 1994, the House Foreign Affairs Committee reported H.J.Res. 416 authorizing the forces in Haiti until March 1, 1995, and providing procedures for a joint resolution to withdraw the forces. On October 6, the House adopted an amended text introduced by Representative Ron Dellums. As passed, H.J.Res. 416 stated the sense of the Congress that the President should have sought congressional approval before deploying U.S. forces to

War Powers Resolution: Presidential Compliance 15

Haiti, supported a prompt and orderly withdrawal as soon as possible, and required a monthly report on Haiti as well as other reports. This same language was also adopted by the Senate on October 6 as S. J. Res. 229, and on October 7 the House passed S.J.Res. 229. President Clinton signed it on October 25, 1994 (P.L. 103-423).

After the U.S. forces began to disarm Haitian forces and President Aristide returned on October 15, 1994, the United States began to withdraw some forces. On March 31, 1995, U.N. peacekeeping forces assumed responsibility for missions previously conducted by U.S. military forces. By September 21, 1995, President Clinton reported the United States had 2,400 military personnel in Haiti as participants in the U.N. Mission in Haiti (UNMIH), and 260 U.S. military personnel assigned to the U.S. Support Group Haiti. On December 5, 1997, President Clinton stated that he intended to keep some military personnel in Haiti, even though United Nations peacekeeping forces were withdrawing. The Pentagon stated that U.S. military personnel in Haiti would be about 500, consisting mainly of engineering and medical units, with a combat element responsible for protecting the U.S. contingent. On March 2, 2004, the President reported to Congress "consistent with the War Powers Resolution" that, on February 29, he had sent about "200 additional U.S. combat-equipped, military personnel from the U.S. Joint Forces Command" to Port- au-Prince, Haiti, for a variety of purposes, including preparing the way for a U.N. Multinational Interim Force, and otherwise supporting U.N. Security Council Resolution 1529 (2004). For further information on Haiti, see CRS Report RL32294, *Haiti: Developments and U.S. Policy Since 1991 and Current Congressional Concerns*, by Maureen Taft-Morales.

Somalia

In Somalia, the participation of U.S. military forces in a U.N. operation to protect humanitarian assistance, which began in December 1992, became increasingly controversial as fighting and casualties increased and objectives appeared to be expanding. On October 7, 1993, President Clinton announced that all U.S. forces would be withdrawn by March 31, 1994, and most forces left by that date. The remaining 58 Marines, who had remained to protect U.S. diplomats, were withdrawn September 15, 1994.

A major issue for Congress was whether to authorize U.S. action in Somalia. On February 4, 1993, the Senate passed S.J.Res. 45 to authorize the

President to use U.S. armed forces pursuant to U.N. Security Council Resolution 794. S.J.Res. 45 stated it was intended to constitute the specific statutory authorization under Section 5(b) of the War Powers Resolution. On May 25, 1993, the House amended and passed S.J.Res. 45. The amendment authorized U.S. forces to remain for one year. S.J.Res. 45 was then sent to the Senate for its concurrence, but the measure did not reach the floor.

As sporadic fighting resulted in the deaths of Somali and U.N. forces, including Americans, controversy over the operation intensified. On September 9, 1993, the Senate adopted an amendment to S. 1298, the Defense Authorization Bill, expressing the sense of Congress that the President by November 15, 1993, should seek and receive congressional authorization for the continued deployment of U.S. forces to Somalia. It asked that the President consult with Congress and report the goals, objectives, and anticipated jurisdiction of the U.S. mission in Somalia by October 15, 1993. On September 29, the House adopted a similar amendment to its bill, H.R. 2401. On October 7, the President consulted with congressional leaders from both parties for over two hours on Somalia policy and also announced that U.S. forces would be withdrawn by March 31, 1994.

On October 15, 1993, the Senate adopted an amendment by Senator Byrd to H.R. 3116, the Defense Department Appropriations Act for FY1 994, cutting off funds for U.S. military operations in Somalia after March 31, 1994, unless the President obtained further spending authority from Congress. The Senate approved the use of military operations only for the protection of American military personnel and bases and for helping maintain the flow of relief aid by giving the U.N. forces security and logistical support. The amendment, which became Section 8151 of P.L. 103-13 9, required U.S. forces in Somalia to remain under the command and control of U.S. commanders. In addition, on November 9, 1993, the House adopted H.Con.Res. 170, using Section 5(c) of the War Powers Resolution to direct the President to remove forces from Somalia by March 31, 1994; sponsors stated it was a non-binding measure, and the Senate did not act on the measure. The Defense Appropriations Act for FY1995 (P.L. 103-335, signed September 30, 1994) prohibited the use of funds for the continuous presence of U.S. forces in Somalia, except for the protection of U.S. personnel, after September 30, 1994.

On November 4, the U.N. Security Council decided to end the U.N. mission in Somalia by March 31, 1995. On March 3, 1995, U.S. forces completed their assistance to United Nations forces evacuating Somalia.

Instances Formally Reported Under the War Powers Resolution

Presidents have submitted 123 reports to Congress as a result of the War Powers Resolution. Of these, President Ford submitted 4, President Carter 1, President Reagan 14, President George H.W. Bush 7, President Clinton 60, and President George W. Bush 37. For a summary of the 111 reports submitted by the Presidents from 1975-2003, see CRS Report RL32267, *The War Powers Resolution: After Thirty-Three Years*, by Richard F. Grimmett. The following is a brief summary of reports submitted by President Bush George W. Bush since January 2004. The reports are submitted to the Speaker of the House as executive communications, and subsequently published on the U.S. government printing office website under House Documents. The full texts of these Presidential reports may be found at [*http://www.gpoaccess. gov/serialset/cdocuments/index.html*].

(112) On January 22, 2004, the President reported to Congress "consistent with the War Powers Resolution" that the United States was continuing to deploy combat equipped military personnel in Bosnia and Herzegovina in support of NATO's Stabilization Force (SFOR) and its peacekeeping efforts in this country. About 1,800 U.S. personnel are participating.

(113) On February 25, 2004, the President reported to Congress "consistent with the War Powers Resolution" that, on February 23, he had sent a combat- equipped "security force" of about "55 U.S. military personnel from the U.S. Joint Forces Command" to Port-au-Prince, Haiti to augment the U.S. Embassy security forces there and to protect American citizens and property in light of the instability created by the armed rebellion in Haiti.

(114) On March 2, 2004, the President reported to Congress "consistent with the War Powers Resolution" that on February 29 he had sent about "200 additional U.S. combat-equipped, military personnel from the U.S. Joint Forces Command" to Port- au-Prince, Haiti for a variety of purposes, including preparing the way for a UN Multinational Interim Force, and otherwise supporting UN Security Council Resolution 1529 (2004). On March 20, 2004, the President sent to Congress "consistent with the War Powers Resolution," a consolidated report giving details of multiple ongoing United States military deployments and operations "in support of the global war on terrorism (including in Afghanistan)," as well as operations in Bosnia and Herzegovina, Kosovo, and Haiti. In this report, the President noted that U.S. anti- terror related activities were underway in Georgia, Djibouti, Kenya,

Ethiopia, Yemen, and Eritrea. He further noted that U.S. combat-equipped military personnel continued to be deployed in Kosovo as part of the NATO-led KFOR (1,900 personnel); in Bosnia and Herzegovina as part of the NATO-led SFOR (about 1,100 personnel); and approximately 1,800 military personnel were deployed in Haiti as part of the U.N. Multinational Interim Force.

(115) On November 4, 2004, the President sent to Congress, "consistent with the War Powers Resolution," a consolidated report giving details of multiple ongoing United States military deployments and operations "in support of the global war on terrorism." These deployments, support or military operations include activities in Afghanistan, Djibouti, as well as Kenya, Ethiopia, Eritrea, Bosnia and Herzegovina, and Kosovo. In this report, the President noted that U.S. anti-terror related activities were underway in Djibouti, Kenya, Ethiopia, Yemen, and Eritrea. He further noted that U.S. combat-equipped military personnel continued to be deployed in Kosovo as part of the NATO-led KFOR (1,800 personnel); and in Bosnia and Herzegovina as part of the NATO-led SFOR (about 1,000 personnel). Meanwhile, he stated that the United States continues to deploy more than 135,000 military personnel in Iraq.

(116) On May 20, 2005, the President sent to Congress "consistent with the War Powers Resolution," a consolidated report giving details of multiple ongoing United States military deployments and operations "in support of the global war on terrorism," as well as operations in Iraq, where currently about 139,000 U.S. military personnel are stationed. U.S. forces are also deployed in Kenya, Ethiopia, Yemen, Eritrea, and Djibouti assisting in "enhancing counter-terrorism capabilities" of these nations. The President further noted that U.S. combat-equipped military personnel continued to be deployed in Kosovo as part of the NATO-led KFOR (1,700 personnel). Approximately 235 U.S. personnel are also deployed in Bosnia and Herzegovina as part of the NATO Headquarters-Sarajevo who assist in defense reform and perform operational tasks, such as counter-terrorism and supporting the International Criminal Court for the Former Yugoslavia.

(117) On December 7, 2005, the President sent to Congress "consistent" with the War Powers Resolution, a consolidated report giving details of multiple ongoing United States military deployments and operations "in support of the global war on terrorism," and in support of the Multinational Force in Iraq, where about 160, 000 U.S. military personnel are deployed. U.S. forces are also deployed in the Horn of Africa region — Kenya, Ethiopia, Yemen, and Djibouti — assisting in "enhancing counter-terrorism

capabilities" of these nations. The President further noted that U.S. combat-equipped military personnel continued to be deployed in Kosovo as part of the NATO-led KFOR (1,700 personnel). Approximately 220 U.S. personnel are also deployed in Bosnia and Herzegovina as part of the NATO Headquarters-Sarajevo who assist in defense reform and perform operational tasks, such as "counterterrorism and supporting the International Criminal Court for the Former Yugoslavia."

(118) On June 15, 2006, the President sent to Congress "consistent" with the War Powers Resolution, a consolidated report giving details of multiple ongoing United States military deployments and operations "in support of the war on terror," and in Kosovo, Bosnia and Herzegovina, and as part of the Multinational Force (MNF) in Iraq. Presently, about 131, 000 military personnel were deployed in Iraq. U.S. forces were also deployed in the Horn of Africa region, and in Djibouti to support necessary operations against al-Qaida and other international terrorists operating in the region. U.S. military personnel continue to support the NATO-led Kosovo Force (KFOR). The current U.S. contribution to KFOR is about 1,700 military personnel. The NATO Headquarters-Sarajevo was established in November 22, 2004 as a successor to its stabilization operations in Bosnia-Herzegovina to continue to assist in implementing the peace agreement. Approximately 250 U.S. personnel are assigned to the NATO Headquarters-Sarajevo who assist in defense reform and perform operational tasks, such as "counter-terrorism and supporting the International Criminal Court for the Former Yugoslavia." On July 18, 2006, the President reported to Congress "consistent" with the War Powers Resolution, that in response to the security threat posed in Lebanon to U.S. Embassy personnel and citizens and designated third country personnel," he had deployed combat-equipped military helicopters and military personnel to Beirut to assist in the departure of the persons under threat from Lebanon. The President noted that additional combat-equipped U.S. military forces may be deployed "to Lebanon, Cyprus and other locations, as necessary." to assist further departures of persons from Lebanon and to provide security. He further stated that once the threat to U.S. citizens and property has ended, the U.S. military forces would redeploy.

(119) On December 15, 2006, the President sent to Congress "consistent" with the War Powers Resolution, a consolidated report giving details of multiple ongoing United States military deployments and operations "in support of the war on terror," in Kosovo, Bosnia and Herzegovina, and as part of the Multinational Force (MNF) in Iraq. Presently, about 134, 000 military personnel are deployed in Iraq. U.S. forces were also deployed in the Horn of

Africa region, and in Djibouti to support necessary operations against al-Qaida and other international terrorists operating in the region, including Yemen. U.S. military personnel continue to support the NATO-led Kosovo Force (KFOR). The current U.S. contribution to KFOR is about 1,700 military personnel. The NATO Headquarters-Sarajevo was established in November 22, 2004 as a successor to its stabilization operations in Bosnia-Herzegovina to continue to assist in implementing the peace agreement. Approximately 100 U.S. personnel are assigned to the NATO Headquarters-Sarajevo who assist in defense reform and perform operational tasks, such as "counter-terrorism and supporting the International Criminal Court for the Former Yugoslavia."

(120) On July 18, 2006, the President reported to Congress "consistent" with theWar Powers Resolution, that in response to the security threat posed in Lebanon toU.S. Embassy personnel and citizens and designated third country personnel," he haddeployed combat-equipped military helicopters and military personnel to Beirut toassist in the departure of the persons under threat from Lebanon. The President notedthat additional combat-equipped U.S. military forces may be deployed "to Lebanon,Cyprus and other locations, as necessary." to assist further departures of persons fromLebanon and to provide security. He further stated that once the threat to U.S.citizens and property has ended, the U.S. military forces would redeploy.

(121) On December 15, 2006, the President sent to Congress "consistent" withthe War Powers Resolution, a consolidated report giving details of multiple ongoingUnited States military deployments and operations "in support of the war on terror,"in Kosovo, Bosnia and Herzegovina, and as part of the Multinational Force (MNF)in Iraq. Presently, about 134, 000 military personnel are deployed in Iraq. U.S. forceswere also deployed in the Horn of Africa region, and in Djibouti to support necessaryoperations against al-Qaida and other international terrorists operating in the region,including Yemen. U.S. military personnel continue to support the NATO-ledKosovo Force (KFOR). The current U.S. contribution to KFOR is about 1,700military personnel. The NATO Headquarters-Sarajevo was established in November22, 2004 as a successor to its stabilization operations in Bosnia-Herzegovina tocontinue to assist in implementing the peace agreement. Approximately 100 U.S.personnel are assigned to the NATO Headquarters-Sarajevo who assist in defensereform and perform operational tasks, such as "counter-terrorism and supporting theInternational Criminal Court for the Former Yugoslavia."

(122) On June 15, 2007, the President sent to Congress "consistent" with the War Powers Resolution, a consolidated report giving details of ongoing United States military deployments and operations "in support of the war on

terror,"and in support of the NATO-led Kosovo Force (KFOR). The President reported that various U.S. "combat-equipped and combat-support forces" were deployed to "a number of locations in the Central, Pacific, European (KFOR), and Southern Command areas of operation" and were engaged in combat operations against al-Qaida terrorists and their supporters. The U.S. is currently "pursuing and engaging remnant al-Qaida and Taliban fighters in Afghanistan." U.S. forces in Afghanistan currently total approximately 25,945. Of this total, "approximately 14,340 are assigned to the International Security Assistance Force (ISAF) in Afghanistan." The U.S. military continues to support peacekeeping operations in Kosovo, specifically the NATO-led Kosovo Force (KFOR). Currently, the U.S. contribution to KFOR in Kosovo is approximately 1,584 military personnel.

(123) On December 14, 2007, the President sent to Congress "consistent with the War Powers Resolution," a consolidated report giving details of ongoing United States military deployments and operations "in support of the war on terror,"and in support of the NATO-led Kosovo Force (KFOR). The President reported that various U.S. "combat-equipped and combat-support forces" were deployed to "a number of locations in the Central, Pacific, European, and Southern Command areas of operation" and were engaged in combat operations against al-Qaida terrorists and their supporters. The United States. is currently "pursuing and engaging remnant alQaida and Taliban fighters in Afghanistan." U.S. forces in Afghanistan currently total approximately 25,900. Of this total, "approximately 15,180 are assigned to the International Security Assistance Force (ISAF) in Afghanistan." The U.S. military continues to support peacekeeping operations in Kosovo, specifically the NATO-led Kosovo Force (KFOR). Currently, the U.S. contribution to KFOR in Kosovo is approximately 1,498 military personnel.

CONSULTATION WITH CONGRESS

Section 3 of the War Powers Resolution requires the President "in every possible instance" to consult with Congress before introducing U.S. armed forces into situations of hostilities and imminent hostilities, and to continue consultations as long as the armed forces remain. A review of instances involving the use of armed forces since passage of the Resolution, noted in this report, indicates there has been very little consultation with Congress under the Resolution when consultation is defined to mean seeking advice prior to a decision to introduce troops. Presidents have met with congressional leaders after the decision to deploy was made but before commencement of operations.

One problem is the interpretation of when consultation is required. The War Powers Resolution established different criteria for consultation than for reporting. Consultation is required only before introducing armed forces into "hostilities or into situations where imminent involvement in hostilities is clearly indicated by the circumstances," the circumstances triggering the time limit. A second problem is the meaning of the term consultation. The executive branch has often taken the view that the consultation requirement has been fulfilled when from the viewpoint of some Members of Congress it has not. The House report on the War Powers Resolution said, "... consultation in this provision means that a decision is pending on a problem and that Members of Congress are being asked by the President for their advice and opinions and, in appropriate circumstances, their approval of action contemplated." A third problem is who represents Congress for consultation purposes. The House version specifically called for consultation between the President and the leadership and appropriate committees. This was changed to less specific wording in final House-Senate conference committee version, to provide some flexibility. Some critics of the existing statute have introduced proposals to specify a consultation group. But Congress has yet to act on such a proposal.

ISSUES FOR CONGRESS

An immediate issue for Congress when the President introduces troops into situations of potential hostilities is whether to invoke Section 4(a)(1) of the War Powers Resolution and trigger a durational limit for the action unless Congress authorizes the forces to remain. If Congress concurs in a President's action, application of the Resolution may be desirable either to legitimize the action and strengthen it by making clear congressional support for the measure or to establish the precedent that the Resolution does apply in such a situation. On the other hand, some may believe it is preferable to leave the President more flexibility of action than is possible under the Resolution. Or some may not wish to have a formal vote on either the issue of applying the Resolution or the merits of utilizing armed forces in that case. If Congress does not concur in an action taken by a president, the Resolution offers a way to terminate it.

A longer-term issue is whether the War Powers Resolution is working or should be amended. Some contend that it has been effective in moderating the President's response to crisis situations because of his awareness that certain actions would trigger its reporting and legislative veto provisions. Or they suggest that it could be effective if the President would comply fully or Congress would invoke its provisions. Others believe it is not accomplishing its objectives and suggest various changes. Some have proposed that the Resolution return to the original Senate-passed version, which would enumerate circumstances in which the President needed no congressional authorization for use of armed forces (namely to respond to or forestall an armed attack against the United States or its forces or to protect U.S. citizens while evacuating them) but prohibit any other use or any permissible use for more than 30 days unless authorized by Congress. Others would replace the automatic requirement for withdrawal of troops after 60 days with expedited procedures for a joint resolution authorizing the action or requiring disengagement. Still others would repeal the Resolution on grounds that it restricts the President's effectiveness in foreign policy or is unconstitutional.

Several Members have suggested establishing a consultative group to meet with the President when military action is being considered. Senators Byrd, Nunn, Warner, and Mitchell introduced S.J.Res. 323 in 1988 and S. 2 in 1989 to establish a permanent consultation group of 18 Members consisting of the leadership and the ranking and minority members of the Committees on Foreign Relations, Armed Services, and Intelligence. The bill would permit an initial consultative process to be limited to a core group of six Members — the majority and minority leaders of both chambers plus the Speaker of the House and President pro tempore of the Senate. On October 28, 1993, House Foreign Affairs Chairman Lee Hamilton introduced H.R. 3405 to establish a congressional consultative group equivalent to the National Security Council. No action was taken on this proposal.

Thus far, however, executive branch officials and congressional leaders, who themselves have varying opinions, have been unable to find mutually acceptable changes in the War Powers Resolution. President Clinton, in Presidential Decision Directive 25 signed May 3, 1994, supported legislation to amend the Resolution along the lines of the Mitchell, Nunn, Byrd, and Warner proposal of 1989, to establish a consultative mechanism and also eliminate the 60-day withdrawal provisions. Although many agreed on the consultation group, supporters of the legislation contended the time limit had been the main flaw in the War Powers Resolution, whereas opponents contended the time limit provided the teeth of the Resolution. The difficulty of reaching consensus in Congress on what action to take is reflected in the fact that in the 104th Congress, only one measure, S. 5, introduced January 4, 1995, by then Majority Leader Dole was the subject of a hearing. S. 5, if enacted, would have repealed most of the existing War Powers Resolution. An effort to repeal most of the War Powers Resolution in the House on June 7, 1995, through an amendment to the Foreign Assistance and State Department Authorization Act for FY1 996-97 (H.R. 1561) by Representative Hyde, failed (201-217). Other than these instances, no other War Powers related legislation was even considered during the 104th Congress.

On March 18, 1998, the House defeated H.Con.Res. 227, a resolution that would have directed the President, pursuant to section 5(c) of the War Powers Resolution to remove United States Armed Forces from the Republic of Bosnia and Herzegovina (H.Rept. 105-442). It was the hope of Representative Tom Campbell, its sponsor, that passage of the resolution could lead to a court case that would address the constitutionality of the War Powers Resolution. On March 31, 1998, the House passed a Supplemental Appropriations bill (H.R. 3579) that would ban use of funds for conduct of offensive operations against Iraq, unless such operations were specifically authorized by law. This provision was dropped in the conference with the Senate. On June 24, 1998, the House passed H.R. 4103, the Defense Department Appropriations bill for FY1999, with a provision by Representative Skaggs that banned the use of funds appropriated or **otherwise made available by this act** "to initiate or conduct offensive military operations by United States Armed Forces except in accordance with the war powers clause of the Constitution (Article 1, Section 8), which vests in Congress the power to declare and authorize war and to take certain specified, related actions." **The Skaggs provision was stricken by the House-Senate** conference committee on H.R. 4103. No further War Powers-related actions were taken by Congress by the adjournment of the 105th Congress.

During the 106th Congress, efforts were made to force the President to seek congressional authority for military operations in Kosovo, leading to votes in the House and Senate on that issue. Subsequently, Representative Tom Campbell and others sued the President in Federal Court in an effort to clarify congressional- Executive authority in this area. A Federal District Court and an Appeals Court refused to decide the case on the merits, instead holding that the plaintiffs lacked standing to sue. On October 2, 2000, the United States Supreme Court, let stand the holding of the U.S. Appeals Court.[1]

During the first session of the 107th Congress, the Congress passed S.J.Res. 23, on September 14, 2001, in the wake of the terrorist attacks against the World Trade Center in New York City, and the Pentagon building in Arlington, Virginia. This legislation, titled the "Authorization for Use of Military Force," passed the Senate by a vote of 98-0; the House of Representatives passed it by a vote of 420-1. This joint resolution authorizes the President "to use all necessary and appropriate force against those nations, organizations, or persons he determines planned, authorized, committed, or aided the terrorist attacks that occurred on September 11, 2001, or harbored such organizations or persons, in order to prevent any future acts of international terrorism against the United States by such nations, organizations or persons." Congress further declared in the joint resolution that "Consistent with section 8(a)(1) of the War Powers resolution," the above language is "intended to constitute specific statutory authorization within the meaning of section 5(b) the War Powers Resolution." S.J.Res. 23 further stated that "Nothing in this resolution supersedes any requirement of the War Powers Resolution." President George W. Bush signed S.J.Res. 23 into law on September 18, 2001 (P.L. 107-40, 115 Stat. 224).[2]

During the second session of the 107th Congress, the Congress passed H.J.Res. 114, the Authorization for the Use of Force Against Iraq Resolution of 2002 (P.L. 107-243). On October 16, 2002, President Bush signed this legislation into law. This statute authorizes the President to use the armed forces of the United States

> as he determines to be necessary and appropriate in order to (1) defend the national security of the United States against the continuing threat posed by Iraq; and (2) enforce all relevant United Nations Security Council resolutions regarding Iraq.

Prior to using force under this statute the President is required to communicate to Congress his determination that the use of diplomatic and other peaceful means will not "adequately protect the United States ... or ... lead to enforcement of all relevant United Nations Security Council resolutions" and that the use of force is "consistent" with the battle against terrorism. The statute also stipulates that it is "intended to constitute specific statutory authorization within the meaning of section 5(b) of the War Powers Resolution." It further requires the President to make periodic reports to Congress "on matters relevant to this joint resolution." Finally, the statute expresses Congress's "support" for the efforts of the President to obtain "prompt and decisive action by the Security Council" to enforce Iraq's compliance with all relevant Security Council resolutions.

P.L. 107-243 clearly confers broad authority on the President to use force. The authority granted is not limited to the implementation of **previously adopted** Security Council resolutions concerning Iraq but includes "all relevant ... resolutions." Thus, it appears to incorporate resolutions concerning Iraq that may be adopted by the Security Council in the future as well as those already adopted. The authority also appears to extend beyond compelling Iraq's disarmament to implementing the full range of concerns expressed in those resolutions. The President's exercise of the authority granted is **not** dependent upon a finding that Iraq was complicit in the attacks of September 11, 2001. Moreover, the authority conferred can be used for the purpose of defending "the national security of the United States against the continuing threat posed by Iraq." On March 19, 2003, President Bush used the authority granted in P.L. 107-243 by launching a military attack against Iraq. The President continues to use that authority for ongoing military operations in Iraq.

End Notes

[1] Campbell v. Clinton, 52 F. Supp. 2d 34 (D.D.C. 1999), *aff'd*, 203 F.3d 19 (D.C. Cir. 2000), *cert. denied*, 531 U.S. 815 (2000).

[2] For details relating to enactment of this authority, see CRS Report RS22357, *Authorization For Use Of Military Force in Response to the 9/11 Attacks (P.L. 107-40): Legislative History*.

In: War Powers Resolution after 34 Years... ISBN: 978-1-60692-787-8
Editors: Jeremiah E. Sanders © 2010 Nova Science Publishers, Inc.

Chapter 2

THE WAR POWERS RESOLUTION: AFTER THIRTY-FOUR YEARS

F. Richard Grimmett
International Security Foreign Affairs, Defense, and Trade Division

SUMMARY

This report discusses and assesses the War Powers Resolution, its application since enactment in 1973, providing detailed background on a variety of cases where it was utilized, or issues of its applicability were raised. It will be revised biannually.

In the post-Cold War world, Presidents have continued to commit U.S. Armed Forces into potential hostilities, sometimes without a specific authorization from Congress. Thus the War Powers Resolution and its purposes continues to be a potential subject of controversy. On June 7, 1995 the House defeated, by a vote of 217-201, an amendment to repeal the central features of the War Powers Resolution that have been deemed unconstitutional byeveryPresident since the law's enactment in 1973. In 1999, after the President committed U.S. military forces to action in Yugoslavia without congressional authorization, Representative Tom Campbell used expedited procedures under the Resolution to force a debate and votes on U.S. military action in Yugoslavia, and later sought, unsuccessfully, through a federal court suit to enforce Presidential compliance with the terms of the War Powers Resolution.

The War Powers Resolution (P.L. 93-148) was passed over the veto of President Nixon on November 7, 1973, to provide procedures for Congress and the President to participate in decisions to send U.S. Armed Forces into hostilities. Section 4(a)(1) requires the President to report to Congress any introduction of U.S. forces into hostilities or imminent hostilities. When such a report is submitted, or is required to be submitted, section 5(b) requires that the use of forces must be terminated within 60 to 90 days unless Congress authorizes such use or extends the time period. Section 3 requires that the **"President in every possible instance shall** consult with Congress before **introducing" U.S. Armed Forces into hostilities or imminent hostilities.**

From 1975 through 2007, Presidents have submitted 123 reports as the result of the War Powers Resolution, but only one, the 1975 *Mayaguez* seizure, cited section 4(a)(1) which triggers the time limit, and in this case the military action was completed and U.S. armed forces had disengaged from the area of conflict when the report was made. The reports submitted by the President since enactment of the War Powers Resolution cover a range of military activities from embassy evacuations to full scale combat military operations, such as the Persian Gulf conflict, and the 2003 war with Iraq, the intervention in Kosovo and the anti-terrorism actions in Afghanistan. In some instances U.S. Armed Forces have been used in hostile situations without formal reports to Congress under the War Powers Resolution. On one occasion, Congress exercised its authority to determine that the requirements of section 4(a)(1) became operative on August 29, 1983, through passage of the Multinational Force in Lebanon Resolution (P.L. 98-119). In 1991 and 2002, Congress authorized, by law, the use of military force against Iraq. In several instances neither the President, Congress, nor the courts have been willing to trigger the War Powers Resolution mechanism.

INTRODUCTION

Under the Constitution, the war powers are divided between Congress and the President. Among other relevant grants, Congress has the power to declare war and raise and support the armed forces (Article I, section 8), while the President is Commander in Chief (Article II, section 2). It is generally agreed that the Commander in Chief role gives the President power to utilize the armed forces to repel attacks against the United States, but there has long been controversy over whether heis constitutionally authorized to send forces into hostilesituations abroad without a declaration of war or other congressional authorization.

Congressional concern about Presidential use of armed forces without congressional authorization intensified after the Korean conflict. During the Vietnam war, Congress searched for a way to assertauthority to decide when the United States should become involved in a war or the armed forces be utilized in circumstances that might lead to hostilities. On November 7, 1973, it passed the War Powers Resolution (P.L. 93-148) over the veto of President Nixon. The main purpose of the Resolution was to establish procedures for both branches to share in decisions that might get the United States involved in war. The drafters sought to circumscribe the President's authority to use armed forces abroad in hostilities or potential hostilities without a declaration of war or other congressional authorization, yet provide enough flexibility to permit him to respond to attack or other emergencies.

The record of the War Powers Resolution since its enactment has been mixed, and after 30 years it remains controversial. Some Members of Congress believe the Resolution has on some occasions served as a restraint on the use of armed forces by Presidents, provided a mode of communication, and given Congress a vehicle for asserting its war powers. Others have sought to amend the Resolution because they believe it has failed to assure a congressional voice in committing U.S. troops to potential conflicts abroad. Others in Congress, along with executive branch officials, contend that the President needs more flexibility in the conduct of foreign policy and that the time limitation in the War Powers Resolution is unconstitutional and impractical. Some have argued for its repeal.

This report examines the provisions of the War Powers Resolution, actual experience in its use from its enactment in 1973 through December 2007, and proposed amendments to it. Appendix A lists instances which Presidents have reported to Congress under the War Powers Resolution, and Appendix B lists representative instances of the use of U.S. armed forces that were not reported.

PROVISIONS OF THE WAR POWERS RESOLUTION
(P.L. 93-148)

Title

Section 1 establishes the title, "The War Powers Resolution." The law is frequently referred to as the "War Powers Act," the title of the measure passed by the Senate. Although the latter is not technically correct, it does serve to emphasize that the War Powers Resolution, embodied in a joint resolution which complies with constitutional requirements for lawmaking, is a law.

Purpose and Policy

Section 2 states the Resolution's purpose and policy, with Section 2(a) citing as the primary purpose to "insure that the collective judgment of both the Congress and the President will apply to the introduction of United States Armed Forces into hostilities, or into situations where imminent involvement in hostilities is clearly indicated by the circumstances, and to the continued use of such forces in hostilities or in such situations."

Section 2(b) points to the Necessary and Proper Clause of the Constitution as the basis for legislation on the war powers. It provides that "Under Article I, section 8, of the Constitution it is specifically provided that Congress shall have the power to make all laws necessary and proper for carrying into execution, not only its own powers but also all other powers vested by the Constitution in the Government of the United States...."

Section 2(c) states the policy that the powers of the President as Commander in Chief to introduce U.S. armed forces into situations of hostilities or imminent hostilities "are exercised only pursuant to —

(1) a declaration of war,
(2) specific statutory authorization, or
(3) a national emergency created by attack upon the United States, its territories or possessions, or its armed forces."

Consultation Requirement

Section 3 of the War Powers Resolution requires the President "in every possible instance" to consult with Congress before introducing U.S. Armed Forces into situations of hostilities and imminent hostilities, and to continue consultations as long as the armed forces remain in such situations. The House report elaborated:

> A considerable amount of attention was given to the definition of **consultation**. Rejected was the notion that consultation should be synonymous with merely being informed. Rather, consultation in this provision means that a decision is pending on a problem and that Members of Congress are being asked by the President for their advice and opinions and, in appropriate circumstances, their approval of action contemplated. Furthermore, for consultation to be meaningful, the President himself must participate and all information relevant to the situation must be made available.[1]

The House version specifically called for consultation between the President and the leadership and appropriate committees. This was changed to less specific wording in conference, however, in order to provide more flexibility.

Reporting Requirements

Section 4 requires the President to report to Congress whenever he introduces U.S. armed forces abroad in certain situations. Of key importance is section 4(a)(1) because it triggers the time limit in section 5(b). Section 4(a)(1) requires reporting within 48 hours, in the absence of a declaration of war or congressional authorization, the introduction of U.S. armed forces "into hostilities or into situations where imminent involvement in hostilities is clearly indicated bythe circumstances."

Some indication of the meaning of hostilities and imminent hostilities is given in the House report on its War Powers bill:

> The word **hostilities** was substituted for the phrase **armed conflict** during the subcommittee drafting process because it was considered to be somewhat broader in scope. In addition to a situation in which fighting actually has begun, **hostilities** also encompasses a state of confrontation in

which no shots havebeen fired but where there is a clear and present danger of armed conflict. **"Imminent hostilities"** denotes a situation in which there is a clear potential either for such a state of confrontation or for actual armed conflict.[2]

Section 4(a)(2) requires the reporting of the introduction of troops "into the territory, airspace or waters of a foreign nation, while equipped for combat, except for deployments which relate solely to supply, replacement, repair, or training of such forces." According to the House report this was to cover

> the initial commitment of troops in situations in which there is no actual fighting but some risk, however small, of the forces being involved in hostilities. A report would be required any time combat military forces were sent to another nation to alter or preserve the existing political status quo or to make the U.S. presence felt. Thus, for example, the dispatch of Marines to Thailand in 1962 and the quarantine of Cuba in the same year would have required Presidential reports. Reports would not be required for routine port supply calls, emergency aid measures, normal training exercises, and other noncombat military activities.[3]

Section 4(a)(3) requires the reporting of the introduction of troops "in numbers which substantially enlarge United StatesArmed Forces equipped for combat already located in a foreign nation." The House report elaborated:

> While the word "substantially" designates a flexible criterion, it is possible to arrive at a common-sense understanding of the numbers involved. A 100% increase in numbers of Marine guards at an embassy — say from 5 to 10 — clearly would not be an occasion for a report. A thousand additional men sent to Europe under present circumstances does not significantly enlarge the total U.S. troop strength of about 300,000 already there. However, the dispatch of 1,000 men to Guantanamo Bay, Cuba, which now has a complement of 4,000 would mean an increase of 25%, which is substantial. Under this circumstance, President Kennedy would have been required to report to Congress in 1962 when he raised the number of U.S. military advisers in Vietnam from 700 to 16,000.[4]

All of the reports under Section 4(a), which are to be submitted to the Speaker of the House and the President pro tempore of the Senate, are to set forth:

(A) the circumstances necessitating the introduction of United States Armed Forces;

(B) the constitutional and legislative authority under which such introduction took place; and

(C) the estimated scope and duration of the hostilities or involvement.

Section 4(b) requires the President to furnish such other information as Congress may request to fulfill its responsibilities relating to committing the nation to war.

Section 4(c) requires the President to report to Congress periodically, and at least every six months, whenever U.S. forces are introduced into hostilities or any other situation in section 4(a).

The objectives of these provisions, the conference report stated, was to "ensure that the Congress by right and as a matter of law will be provided with all the information it requires to carry out its constitutional responsibilities with respect to committingtheNation to war and to the use of United States Armed Forces abroad."[5]

Congressional Action

Section 5(a) deals with congressional procedures for receipt of a report under section 4(a)(1). It provides that if a report is transmitted during a congressional adjournment, the Speaker of the House and the President pro tempore of the Senate, when they deem it advisable or if petitioned by at least 30% of the Members of their respective Houses, shall jointly request the President to convene Congress in order to consider the report and take appropriate action.

Section 5(b) was intended to provide teeth for the War Powers Resolution. After areport "is submitted or is required to be submitted pursuant to section 4(a)(1), whichever is earlier", section 5(b) requires the President to terminate the use of U.S. Armed Forces after 60 days unless Congress (1) has declared war or authorized the action; (2) has extended the period by law; or (3) is physically unable to meet as a result of an armed attack on the United States. The 60 days can be extended for 30 days by the President if he certifies that "unavoidable military necessity respecting the safety of United States Armed Forces" requires their continued use in the course of bringing about their removal.

Section 5(c) requires the President to remove the forces at any time if Congress so directs by concurrent resolution; the effectiveness of this subsection is uncertain because of the 1983 Supreme Court decision on the legislative veto. It is discussed in Part II of this report.

Priority Procedures

Section 6 establishes expedited procedures for congressional consideration of a joint resolution or bill introduced to authorize the use of armed forces under section 5 (b). They provide for:

(a) A referral to the House Foreign Affairs [International Relations] or Senate Foreign Relations Committee, the committee to report one measure not later than 24 calendar days before the expiration of the 60 day period, unless the relevant House determines otherwise by a vote;

(b) The reported measure to become the pending business of the relevant House and be voted on within three calendar days, unless that House determines otherwise by vote; in the Senate the debate is to be equally divided between proponents and opponents;

(c) A measure passed by one House to be referred to the relevant committee of the other House and reported out not later than 14 calendar days before the expiration of the 60 dayperiod, the reported bill to become the pending business of that House and be voted on within 3 calendar days unless determined otherwise by a vote;

(d) Conferees to file a report not later than four calendar days before the expiration of the 60 day period. If they cannot agree within 48 hours, the conferees are to report back in disagreement, and such report is to be acted on by both Houses not later than the expiration of the 60 day period.

Section 7 establishes similar priority procedures for a concurrent resolution to withdraw forces under section 5(c). For a recent use of these procedures see the section on the legislative veto, below.

Interpretive Provisions

Section 8 sets forth certain interpretations relating to the Resolution. Section 8(a) states that authority to introduce armed forces is not to be inferred from any provision of law or treaty unless it specifically authorizes the introduction of armed forces into hostilities or potential hostilities and states that it is "intended to constitute specific statutory authorization within the meaning of this joint resolution." This language was derived from a Senate measure and was intended to prevent a security treaty or military appropriations act from being used to authorize the introduction of troops. It was also aimed against using a broad resolution like the Tonkin Gulf Resolution[6] to justify hostilities abroad. This resolution had stated that the United States was prepared to take all necessary steps, including use of armed force, to assist certain nations, and it was cited by Presidents and many Members as congressional authorization for the Vietnam war.

Section 8(b) states that further specific statutory authorization is not required

> to permit members of United States Armed Forces to participate jointly with members of the armed forces of one or more foreign countries in the headquarters operations of high-level military commands which were established prior to the date of enactment of this joint resolution and pursuant to the United Nations Charter or any treaty ratified by the United States prior to such date.

This section was added by the Senate to make clear that the resolution did not prevent U.S. forces from participating in certain joint military exercises with allied or friendly organizations or countries. The conference report stated that the "high-level" military commands meant the North Atlantic Treaty Organization, (NATO), the North American Air Defense Command (NORAD) and the United Nations command in Korea.

Section 8(c) defines the introduction of armed forces to include the assignment of armed forces to accompany regular or irregular military forces of other countries when engaged, or potentially engaged, in hostilities. The conference report on the War Powers Resolution explained that this was language modified from a Senate provision requiring specific statutory authorization for assigning members of the Armed Forces for such purposes. The report of the Senate Foreign Relations Committee on its bill said:

The purpose of this provision is to prevent secret, unauthorized military support activities and to prevent a repetition of many of the most controversial and regrettable actions in Indochina. The ever deepening ground combat involvement of the United States in South Vietnam began with the assignment of U.S. "advisers" to accompany South Vietnamese units on combat patrols; and in Laos, secretly and without congressional authorization, U.S. "advisers" were deeply engaged in the war in northern Laos.[7]

Section 8(d) states that nothing in the Resolution is intended to alter the constitutional authority of either the Congress or the President. It also specifies that nothingis to be construed as granting any authority to introduce troops that would not exist in the absence of the Resolution. The House report said that this provision was to help insure the constitutionality of the Resolution by making it clear that nothing in it could be interpreted as changing the powers delegated by the Constitution.

Section 9 is a separability clause, stating that if any provision or its application is found invalid, the remainder of the Resolution is not to be affected.

CONSTITUTIONAL QUESTIONS RAISED

From its inception, the War Powers Resolution was controversial because it operated on the national war powers, powers divided by the Constitution in no definitive fashion between the President and Congress. Congress adopted the resolution in response to the perception that Presidents had assumed more authority to send forces into hostilities than the framers of the Constitution had intended for the Commander-in-Chief. President Nixon in his veto message challenged the constitutionality of the essence of the War Powers Resolution, and particularly two provisions.[8] He argued that the legislative veto provision, permitting Congress to direct the withdrawal of troops by concurrent resolution, was unconstitutional. He also argued that the provision requiring withdrawal of troops after 60-90 days unless Congress passed legislation authorizing such use was unconstitutional because it checked Presidential powers without affirmative congressional action. Every President since the enactment of the War Powers Resolution has taken the position that it is an unconstitutional infringement on the President's authority as Commander-in-Chief.

War Powers of President and Congress

The heart of the challenge to the constitutionality of theWar Powers Resolution rests on differing interpretations by the two branches of the respective war powers of the President and Congress. These differing interpretations, especially the assertions of Presidential authority to send forces into hostile situations without a declaration of war or other authorization by Congress, were the reason for the enactment of the Resolution.

The congressional view was that the framers of the Constitution gave Congress the power to declare war, meaning the ultimate decision whether or not to enter a war. Most Members of Congress agreed that the President as Commander in Chief had power to lead the U.S. forces once the decision to wage war had been made, to defend the nation against an attack, and perhaps in some instances to take other action such as rescuing American citizens. But, in this view, he did not have the power to commit armed forces to war. Bythe early 1970s, the congressional majority view was that the constitutional balance of war powers had swung too far toward the President and needed to be corrected. Opponents argued that Congress always held the power to forbid or terminate U.S. military action by statute or refusal of appropriations, and that without the clear will to act the War Powers Resolution would be ineffective.

In his veto message, President Nixon said the Resolution would impose restrictions upon the authority of the President which would be dangerous to the safety of the Nation and "attempt to take away, by a mere legislative act, authorities which the President has properly exercised under the Constitution for almost 200 years."

The War Powers Resolution in section 2(c) recognized the constitutional powers of the President as Commander-in-Chief to introduce forces into hostilities or imminent hostilities as "exercised only pursuant to (1) a declaration of war, (2) specific statutory authorization, or (3) a national emergency created by attack upon the United States, its territories or possessions, or its armed forces." The executive branch has contended that the President has much broader authority to use forces, including for such purposes as to rescue American citizens abroad, rescue foreign nationals where such action facilitates the rescue of U.S. citizens, protect U.S. Embassies and legations, suppress civil insurrection, implement the terms of an armistice or cease-fire involving the United States, and carry out the terms of security commitments contained in treaties.[9]

Legislative Veto

On June 23, 1983, the Supreme Court in *INS* v. *Chadha*, ruled unconstitutional the legislative veto provision in section 244(c)(2) of the Immigration and Nationality Act.[10] Although the case involved the use of a one-House legislative veto, the decision cast doubt on the validity of any legislative veto device that was not presented to the President for signature. The Court held that to accomplish what the House attempted to do in the *Chadha* case "requires action in conformity with the express procedures of the Constitution's prescription for legislative action: passage by a majority of both Houses and presentment to the President." On July 6, 1983, the Supreme Court affirmed a lower court's decision striking down a provision in another law[11] that permitted Congress to disapprove by concurrent (two-House) resolution.[12]

Since section 5(c) requires forces to be removed by the President if Congress so directs by a concurrent resolution, it is constitutionally suspect under the reasoning applied by the Court.[13] A concurrent resolution is adopted by both chambers, but it does not require presentment to the President for signature or veto. Some legal analysts contend, nevertheless, that the War Powers Resolution is in a unique category which differs from statutes containing a legislative veto over delegated authorities.[14] Perhaps more important, some observers contend, if a majority of both Houses ever voted to withdraw U.S. forces, the President would be unlikely to continue the action for long, and Congress could withhold appropriations to finance further action. Because the War Powers Resolution contains a separability clause in section 9, most analysts take the view that the remainder of the joint resolution would not be affected even if section 5(c) were found unconstitutional.[15]

Congress has taken action to fill the gap left by the possible invalidity of the concurrent resolution mechanism for the withdrawal of troops. On October 20, 1983, the Senate voted to amend the War Powers Resolution by substituting a joint resolution, which requires presentment to the President, for the concurrent resolution in section 5(c), and providing that it would be handled under the expedited procedures in section 7. The House and Senate conferees agreed not to amend the War Powers Resolution itself, but to adopt a free standing measure relating to the withdrawal of troops. The measure, which became law, provided that any joint resolution or bill to require the removal of U.S. armed forces engaged in hostilities outside the United States without a declaration of war or specific statutory authorization would be considered in accordance with the expedited procedures of section 601(b) of the International Security and Arms Export Control Act of 1976,[16] except that it would be amendable and debate on a veto limited to 20 hours.[17] The priority procedures embraced by this provision applied in the Senate only. Handling of such a joint resolution by the House was left to that Chamber's discretion.

House Members attempted to use section 5(c) to obtain a withdrawal of forces from Somalia. On October 22, 1993, Representative Benjamin Gilman introduced H.Con.Res. 170, pursuant to section 5(c) of the War Powers Resolution, directing the President to remove U.S. Armed Forces from Somalia by January 31, 1994. Using the expedited procedures called for in section 5(c), the Foreign Affairs Committee amended the date of withdrawal to March 31, 1994, (the date the President had already agreed to withdraw the forces), and the House adopted H.Con.Res. 170. The Foreign Affairs Committee reported:[18]

> Despite such genuine constitutionality questions, the committee acted in accordance with the expedited procedures in section 7. The committee action was premised on a determination that neither individual Members of Congress nor Committees of Congress should make unilateral judgments about the constitutionality of provisions of law.

Despite the use of the phrase "directs the President", the sponsor of the resolution and Speaker of the House Thomas Foley expressed the view that because of the *Chadha* decision, the resolution would be non-binding. The March 31, 1994, withdrawal date was later enacted as section 8151 of P.L. 103-139, signed November 11, 1993.

Automatic Withdrawal Provision

The automatic withdrawal provision has become perhaps the most controversial provision of the War Powers Resolution. Section 5(b) requires the President to withdraw U.S. forces from hostilities within 60-90 days after a report is submitted or required to be submitted under section 4(a)(1). The triggering of the time limit has been a major factor in the reluctance of Presidents to report, or Congress to insist upon a report, under section 4(a)(1).

Drafters of the War Powers Resolution included a time limit to provide some teeth for Congress, in the event a President assumed a power to act from provisions of resolutions, treaties, or the Constitution which did not constitute an explicit authorization. The Senate report called the time limit "the heart and core" of the bill that "represents, in an historic sense, a restoration of theconstitutional balance which has been distorted by practice in our history and, climatically, in recent decades."[19] The House report emphasized that the Resolution did not grant the President any new authority or any freedom of action during the time limits that he did not alreadyhave.

Administration officials have objected that the provision would require the withdrawal of U.S. forces simply because of congressional inaction during an arbitrary period. Since the resolution recognizes that the President has independent authority to use armed forces in certain circumstances, they state, "on what basis can Congress seek to terminate such independent authority by the mere passage of time?"[20] In addition, they argue, the imposition of a deadline interferes with successful action, signals a divided nation and lack of resolve, gives the enemy a basis for hoping that the President will be forced by domestic opponents to stop an action, and increases risk to U.S. forces in the field. The issue has not been dealt with by the courts.

MAJOR CASES AND ISSUES PRIOR TO THE PERSIAN GULF WAR

Perceptions of the War Powers Resolution tended to be set during the Cold War. During the 1970s the issues revolved largely around the adequacy of consultation. The 1980s raised more serious issues of Presidential compliance and congressional willingness to use the War Powers Resolution to restrain Presidential action. With regard to Lebanon in 1983, Congress itself invoked the War Powers Resolution, but in the 1987-1988 Persian Gulf tanker war Congress chose not to do so. Following is a summary of major U.S. military actions and the issues they raised relating to the War Powers Resolution from its enactment in 1973 to August 1990.[21]

Vietnam Evacuations and Mayaguez: What Is Consultation?

As the Vietnam war ended, on three occasions, in April 1975, President Ford used U.S. forces to help evacuate American citizens and foreign nationals. In addition, in May 1975 President Ford ordered the retaking of a U.S. merchant vessel, the *SS Mayaguez* which had been seized by Cambodian naval patrol vessels. All four actions were reported to Congress citing the War Powers Resolution. The report on the Mayaguez recapture was the only War

Powers report to date to specifically cite section 4(a)(1), but the question of the time limit was moot because the action was over by the time the report was filed.

Among the problems revealed by these first four cases were differences of opinion between the two branches on the meaning of consultation. The Ford Administration held that it had met the consultation requirement because the President had directed that congressional leaders be notified prior to the actual commencement of the introduction of armed forces. The prevailing congressional view was that consultation meant that the President seek congressional opinion, and take it into account, prior to making a decision to commit armed forces.[22]

Iran Hostage Rescue Attempt: Is Consultation Always Necessary and Possible?

After an unsuccessful attempt on April 24, 1980, to rescue American hostages being held in Iran, President Carter submitted a report to Congress to meet the requirements of the War Powers Resolution, but he did not consult in advance. The Administration took the position that consultation was not required because the mission was a rescue attempt, not an act of force or aggression against Iran. In addition, the Administration contended that consultation was not possible or required because the mission depended upon total surprise.

Some Members of Congress complained about the lack of consultation, especially because legislative-executive meetings had been going on since the Iranian crisis had begun the previous year. Just before the rescue attempt, the Senate Foreign Relations Committee had sent a letter to Secretary of State Cyrus Vance requesting formal consultations under the War Powers Resolution. Moreover, shortly before the rescue attempt, the President outlined plans for a rescue attempt to Senate Majority Leader Robert Byrd but did not say it had begun. Senate Foreign Relations Committee Chairman Frank Church stressed as guidelines for the future: (1) consultation required giving Congress an opportunity to participate in the decision making process, not just informing Congress that an operation was underway; and (2) the judgment could not be made unilaterally but should be made by the President and Congress.[23]

El Salvador: When Are Military Advisers in Imminent Hostilities?

One of the first cases to generate substantial controversy because it was never reported under the War Powers Resolution was the dispatch of U.S. militaryadvisers to El Salvador. At the end of February 1981, the Department of State announced the dispatch of 20 additional military advisers to El Salvador to aid its government against guerilla warfare. There were already 19 military advisers in El Salvador sent by the Carter Administration. The Reagan Administration said the insurgents were organized and armed by Soviet bloc countries, particularly Cuba. By March 14, the Administration had authorized a total of 54 advisers, including experts in combat training.

The President did not report the situation under the War Powers Resolution. A State Department memorandum said a report was not required because the U.S. personnel were not being introduced into hostilities or situations of imminent hostilities. The memorandum asserted that if a change in circumstances occurred that raised the prospect of imminent hostilities, the Resolution would be complied with. A justification for not reporting under section 4(a)(2) was that the military personnel being introduced were not equipped for combat.[24] They would, it was maintained, carry only personal sidearms which they were authorized to use only in their own defense or the defense of other Americans.

The State Department held that section 8(c) of the War Powers Resolution was not intended to require a report when U.S. military personnel might be involved in training foreign military personnel, if there were no imminent involvement of U.S. personnel in hostilities. In the case of El Salvador, the memorandum said, U.S. military personnel "will not act as combat advisors, and will not accompany Salvadoran forces in combat, on operational patrols, or in any other situation where combat is likely."

On May 1, 1981, eleven Members of Congress challenged the President's action by filing suit on grounds that he had violated the Constitution and the War Powers Resolution by sending the advisers to El Salvador. Eventually there were 29 co-plaintiffs, but by June 18, 1981, an equal number of Members (13 Senators and 16 Representatives) filed a motion to intervene in the suit, contending that a number of legislative measures were then pending before Congress and that Congress had ample opportunity to vote to end military assistance to El Salvador if it wished.

On October 4, 1982, U.S. District Court Judge Joyce Hens Green dismissed the suit. She ruled that Congress, not the court, must resolve the question of whether the U.S. forces in El Salvador were involved in a hostile or potentially hostile situation. Whiletheremight be situations in which acourt could conclude that U.S. forces were involved in hostilities, she ruled, the "subtleties of fact-finding in this situation should be left to the political branches." She noted that Congress had taken no action to show it believed the President's decision was subject to the War Powers Resolution.[25] On November 18, 1983, a Federal circuit court affirmed the dismissal and on June 8, 1984, the Supreme Court declined consideration of an appeal of that decision.[26]

As the involvement continued and casualties occurred among the U.S. military advisers, various legislative proposals relating to the War Powers Resolution and El Salvador were introduced. Some proposals required a specific authorization prior to the introduction of U.S. forces into hostilities or combat in El Salvador.[27] Other proposals declared that the commitment of U.S. Armed Forces in El Salvador necessitated compliance with section 4(a) of the War Powers Resolution, requiring the President to submit a report.[28]

Neither approach was adopted in legislation, but the Senate Foreign Relations Committee reported that the President had "a clear obligation under the War Powers Resolution to consult with Congress prior to any future decision to commit combat forces to El Salvador."[29] On July 26, 1983, the House rejected an amendment to the Defense Authorization bill (H.R. 2969) to limit the number of active duty military advisers in El Salvador to 55, unless the President reported any increase above that level under section 4(a)(1) of the War Powers Resolution.[30] Nevertheless, the Administration in practice kept the number of trainers at 55.

HONDURAS: WHEN ARE MILITARY EXERCISES MORE THAN TRAINING?

Militaryexercises in Honduras in 1983 and subsequent years raised the question of when military exercises should be reported under the War Powers Resolution. Section 4(a)(2) requires the reporting of introduction of troops equipped for combat, but exempts deployments which relate solely to training.

On July 27, 1983, President Reagan announced "joint training exercises" planned for Central America and the Caribbean. The first contingent of U.S. troops landed in Honduras on August 8, 1983, and the series of ground and ocean exercises continued for several years, involving thousands of ground troops plus warships and fighter planes.

The President did not report the exercises under the War Powers Resolution. He characterized the maneuvers as routine and said the United States had been regularly conducting joint exercises with Latin American countries since 1965. Some Members of Congress, on the other hand, contended that the exercises were part of a policy to support the rebels or "contras" fighting the Sandinista Government of Nicaragua, threatening that government, and increased the possibility of U.S. military involvement in hostilities in Central America.

Several Members of Congress called for reporting the actions under the War Powers Resolution, but some sought other vehicles for congressional control. In 1982, the Boland amendment to the Defense Appropriations Act had already prohibited use of funds to overthrow the Government of Nicaragua or provoke a military exchange between Nicaragua or Honduras.[31] Variations of this amendment followed in subsequent years. After press reports in 1985 that the option of invading Nicaragua was being discussed, the Defense Authorization Act for Fiscal Year 1986 stated the sense of Congress that U.S. armed forces should not be introduced into or over Nicaragua for combat.[32] In 1986, after U.S. helicopters ferried Honduran troops to the Nicaraguan border area, Congress prohibited U.S. personnel from participating in assistance within land areas of Honduras and Costa Rica within 120 miles of the Nicaraguan border, or from entering Nicaragua to provide military advice or support to paramilitary groups operating in that country.[33] Gradually the issue died with peace agreements in the region and the electoral defeat of the Sandinista regime in Nicaragua in 1990.

Lebanon: How Can Congress Invoke the War Powers Resolution?

The War Powers Resolution faced a major testwhen Marines senttoparticipate in a Multinational Force in Lebanon in 1982 became the targets of hostile fire in August 1983. During this period President Reagan filed three reports under the War Powers Resolution, but he did not report under section 4(a)(1) that the forces were being introduced into hostilities or imminent hostilities, thus triggering the 60-90 day time limit.

On September 29, 1983, Congress passed the Multinational Force in Lebanon Resolution determining that the requirements of section 4(a)(1) of the

War Powers Resolution became operative on August 29, 1983.[34] In the same resolution, Congress authorized the continued participation of the Marines in the Multinational Force for 18 months. The resolution was a compromise between Congress and the President. Congress obtained the President's signature on legislation invoking the War Powers Resolution for the first time, but the price for this concession was a congressional authorization for the U.S. troops to remain in Lebanon for 18 months.

The events began on July 6, 1982, when President Reagan announced he would send a small contingent of U.S. troops to a multinational force for temporary peacekeeping in Lebanon. Chairman of the House Foreign Affairs Committee Clement Zablocki wrote President Reagan that if such a force were sent, the United States would be introducing forces into imminent hostilities and a report under section 4(a)(1) would be required. When the forces began to land on August 25, President Reagan reported but did not cite section 4(a)(1) and said the agreement with Lebanon ruled out any combat responsibilities. After overseeing the departure of the Palestine Liberation Organization force, the Marines in the first Multinational Force left Lebanon on September 10, 1982.

The second dispatch of Marines to Lebanon began on September 20, 1982. President Reagan announced that the United States, France, and Italy had agreed to form a new multinational force to return to Lebanon for a limited period of time to help maintain order until the lawful authorities in Lebanon could discharge those duties. The action followed three events that took place after the withdrawal of the first group of Marines: the assassination of Lebanon President-elect Bashir Gemayel, the entry of Israeli forces into West Beirut, and the massacre of Palestinian civilians by Lebanese Christian militiamen.

On September 29, 1982, President Reagan submitted a reportthat 1,200 Marines had begun to arrive in Beirut, but again he did not cite section 4(a)(1), saying instead that the American force would not engage in combat. As a result of incidents in which Marines were killed or wounded, there was again controversy in Congress on whether the President's report should have been filed under section 4(a)(1). In mid-1983 Congress passed the Lebanon Emergency Assistance Act of 1983 requiring statutory authorization for any substantial expansion in the number or role of U.S. Armed Forces in Lebanon. It also included Section 4(b) that stated:

> Nothing in this section is intended to modify, limit, or suspend any of the standards and procedures prescribed by the War Powers Resolution of 1983.[35]

President Reagan reported on the Lebanon situation for the third time on August 30, 1983, still not citing section 4(a)(1), after fighting broke out between various factions in Lebanon and two Marines were killed.

The level of fighting heightened, and as the Marine casualties increased and the action enlarged, there were more calls in Congress for invocation of the War Powers Resolution. Several Members of Congress said the situation had changed since the President's first report and introduced legislation that took various approaches. Senator Charles Mathias introduced S.J.Res. 159 stating that the time limit specified in the War Powers Resolution had begun on August 31, 1983, and authorizing the forces to remain in Lebanon for a period of 120 days after the expiration of the 60-day period. Representative Thomas Downey introduced H.J.Res. 348 directing the President to report under section 4(a)(1) of the War Powers Resolution. Senator Robert Byrd introduced S.J.Res. 163 finding that section 4(a)(1) of the war powers resolution applied to the present circumstances in Lebanon. The House Appropriations Committee approved an amendment to the continuing resolution for FY1984 (H.J.Res. 367), sponsored by Representative Clarence Long, providing that after 60 days, funds could not be "obligated or expended for peacekeeping activities in Lebanon by United States Armed Forces," unless the President had submitted a report under section 4(a)(1) of the War Powers Resolution. A similar amendment was later rejected by the full body, but it reminded the Administration of possible congressional actions.

On September 20, congressional leaders and President Reagan agreed on a compromise resolution invoking section 4(a)(1) and authorizing the Marines to remain for 18 months. The resolution became the first legislation to be handled under the expedited procedures of the War Powers Resolution. On September 28, the House passed H.J.Res. 364 by a vote of 270 to 161. After three days of debate, on September 29, the Senate passed S.J.Res. 159 by a vote of 54 to 46. The House accepted the Senate bill by a vote of 253 to 156. As passed, the resolution contained four occurrences that would terminate the authorization before eighteen months: (1) the withdrawal of all foreign forces from Lebanon, unless the President certified continued U.S. participation was required to accomplish specified purposes; (2) the assumption by the United Nations or the Government of Lebanon of the responsibilities of the Multinational Force; (3) the implementation of other effective security arrangements; or (4) the withdrawal of all other countries from participation in the Multinational Force.[36]

Shortly afterward, on October 23, 1983, 241 U.S. Marines in Lebanon were killed by a suicide truck bombing, bringing new questions in Congress and U.S. public opinion about U.S. participation. On February 7, 1984, President Reagan announced the Marines would be redeployed and on, March 30, 1984, reported to Congress that U.S. participation in the Multinational Force in Lebanon had ended.

Grenada: Do the Expedited Procedures Work?

On October 25, 1983, President Reagan reported to Congress "consistent with" the War Powers Resolution that he had ordered a landingof approximately 1900 U.S. Army and Marine Corps personnel in Grenada. He said that the action was in response to a request from the Organization of Eastern Caribbean States which had formed a collective security force to restore order in Grenada, where anarchic conditions had developed, and to protect the lives of U.S. citizens.

Many Members of Congress contended that the President should have cited section 4(a)(1) of the War Powers Resolution, which would have triggered the 60-90 day time limitation. On November 1, 1983, the House supported this interpretation when it adopted, by a vote of 403-23, H.J Res. 402 declaring that the requirements of section 4(a)(1) had become operative on October 25. The Senate did not act on this measure and a conference was not held. The Senate had adopted a similar measure on October 28 by a vote of 64 to 20, but on November 17 the provision was deleted in the conference report on the debt limit bill to which it was attached.[37] Thus both Houses had voted to invoke section 4(a)(1), but the legislation was not completed.

On November 17, White House spokesman Larry Speakes said the Administration had indicated that there was no need for action as the combat troops would be out within the 60-90 day time period. Speaker Thomas O'Neill took the position that, whether or not Congress passed specific legislation, the War Powers Resolution had become operative on October 25. By December 15, 1983, all U.S. combat troops had been removed from Grenada.

Eleven Members of Congress filed a suit challenging the constitutionality of President Reagan's invasion of Grenada. A district judge held that courts should not decidesuchcases unless the entire Congress used the institutional remediesavailable to it.[38] An appellate court subsequently held that the issue was moot because the invasion had been ended.[39]

Libya: Should Congress Help Decide on Raids to Undertake in Response to International Terrorism?

The use of U.S. forces against Libya in 1986 focused attention on the application of the War Powers Resolution to use of military force against international terrorism.

Tensions between the United States and Libya under the leadership of Col. Muammar Qadhafi had been mounting for several years, particularly after terrorist incidents at the Rome and Vienna airports on December 27, 1985. On January 7, 1986, President Reagan said that the Rome and Vienna incidents were the latest in a series of brutal terrorist acts committed with Qadhafi's backing that constituted armed aggression against the United States.

The War Powers issue was first raised on March 24, 1986, when Libyan forces fired missiles at U.S. aircraft operating in the Gulf of Sidra. In response, the United States fired missiles at Libyan vessels and at Sirte, the Libyan missile site involved. The U.S. presence in the Gulf of Sidra, an area claimed by Libya, was justified as an exercise to maintain freedom of the seas, but it was widely considered a response to terrorist activities.

Subsequently, on April 5, 1986, a terrorist bombing of a discotheque in West Berlin occurred and an American soldier was killed. On April 14 President Reagan announced there was irrefutable evidence that Libya had been responsible, and U.S. Air Force planes had conducted bombing strikes on headquarters, terrorist facilities, and military installations in Libya in response.

The President reported both cases to Congress although the report on the bombing did not cite section 4(a)(1) and the Gulf of Sidra report did not mention the War Powers Resolution at all. Since the actions were short lived, there was no issue of force withdrawal, but several Members introduced bills to amend the War Powers Resolution. One bill called for improving consultation by establishing a special consultative group in Congress.[40] Others called for strengthening the President's hand in combating terrorism by authorizing the President, notwithstanding any other provision of law, to use all measures he deems necessary to protect U.S. persons against terrorist threats.[41]

Persian Gulf, 1987: When Are Hostilities Imminent?

The War Powers Resolution became an issue in activities in the Persian Gulf after an Iraqi aircraft fired a missile on the *USS Stark* on May 17, 1987, killing 37 U.S. sailors. The attack broached the question of whether the Iran-Iraq war had made the Persian Gulf an area of hostilities or imminent hostilities for U.S. forces. Shortly afterwards, the U.S. adoption of a policy of reflagging and providing a naval escort of Kuwaiti oil tankers through the Persian Gulf raised full force the question of whether U.S. policy was risking involvement in war without congressional authorization. During 1987 U.S. Naval forces operating in the Gulf increased to 11 major warships, 6 minesweepers, and over a dozen small patrol boats, and a battleship-led formation was sent to the Northern Arabian Sea and Indian Ocean to augment an aircraft carrier battle group already there.

For several months the President did not report any of the deployments or military incidents under the War Powers Resolution, although on May 20, 1987, after the *Stark* incident, Secretary of State Shultz submitted a report similar to previous ones consistent with War Powers provisions, but not mentioning the Resolution. No reports were submitted after the *USS Bridgeton* struck a mine on July 24, 1987, or the U.S.-chartered *Texaco-Caribbean* struck a mine on August 10 and a U.S. F-14 fighter plane fired two missiles at an Iranian aircraft perceived as threatening.

Later, however, after various military incidents on September 23, 1987, and growing congressional concern, the President began submitting reports "consistent with" the War Powers Resolution and on July 13, 1988, submitted the sixth report relating to the Persian Gulf.[42] None of the reports were submitted under section 4(a)(1) or acknowledged that U.S. forces had been introduced into hostilities or imminent hostilities. The Reagan administration contended that the military incidents in the Persian Gulf, or isolated incidents involving defensive reactions, did not add up to hostilities or imminent hostilities as envisaged in the War Powers Resolution. It held that "imminent danger" pay which was announced for military personnel in the Persian Gulf on August 27, 1987, did not trigger section 4 (a)(1). Standards for danger pay, namely, "subject to the threat of physical harm or danger on the basis of civil insurrection, civil war, terrorism, or wartime conditions," were broader than for hostilities of the War Powers Resolution, and had been drafted to be available in situations to which the War Powers Resolution did not apply. [43]

Some Members of Congress contended that if the President did not report under section 4(a)(1), Congress itself should declare such a report should have been submitted, as it had in the Multinational Force in Lebanon Resolution. Several resolutions to this effect were introduced, some authorizing the forces to remain, but none were passed.[44] The decisive votes on the subject took place in the Senate. On September 18, 1987, the Senate voted 50-41 to table an amendment to the Defense authorization bill (S. 1174) to apply the provisions of the War Powers Resolution. The Senate also sustained points of order against consideration of S.J.Res. 217, which would have invoked the War Powers Resolution, on December 4, 1987, and a similar bill the following year, S.J.Res. 305, on June 6, 1988.

The Senate opted for a different approach, which was to use legislation to assure a congressional role in the Persian Gulf policy without invoking the War Powers Resolution. Early in the situation, both Chambers passed measures requiring the Secretary of Defense to submit a report to Congress prior to the implementation of any agreement between the United States and Kuwait for U.S. military protection of Kuwaiti shipping, and such a report was submitted June 15, 1987. Later, the Senate passed a measure that called for a comprehensive report by the President within 30 days and provided expedited procedures for a joint resolution on the subject after an additional 30 days.[45] The House did not take action on the bill.

As in the case of El Salvador, some Members took the War Powers issue to court. On August 7, 1987, Representative Lowry and 110 other Members of Congress filed suit in the U.S. District Court for the District of Columbia, asking the court to declare that a report was required under section 4(a)(1). On December 18, 1987, the court dismissed the suit, holding it was a nonjusticiable political question, and that the plaintiffs' dispute was "primarily with fellow legislators."[46]

Compliance with the consultation requirement was also an issue. The Administration developed its plan for reflagging and offered it to Kuwait on March 7, 1987, prior to discussing the plan with Members of Congress. A June 15, 1987, report to Congress by the Secretary of Defense stated on the reflagging policy, "As soon as Kuwait indicated its acceptance of our offer, we began consultations with Congress which are still ongoing."[47] This was too late for congressional views to be weighed in on the initial decision, after which it became more difficult to alter the policy. Subsequently, however, considerable consultation developed and the President met with various congressional leaders prior to some actions such as the retaliatory actions in April 1988 against an Iranian oil platform involved in mine-laying.

With recurring military incidents, some Members of Congress took the position that the War Powers Resolution was not being complied with, unless the President reported under section 4(a)(1) or Congress itself voted to invoke the Resolution. Other Members contended the Resolution was working by serving as a restraint on the President, who was now submitting reports and consulting with Congress.[48] Still other Members suggested the Persian Gulf situation was demonstrating the need to amend the War Powers Resolution.

As a result of the Persian Gulf situation, in the summer of 1988 both the House Foreign Affairs Committee and the Senate Foreign Relations Committee, which established a Special Subcommittee on War Powers, undertook extensive assessments of the War Powers Resolution. Interest in the issue waned after a cease-fire between Iran and Iraq began on August 20, 1988, and the United States reduced its forces in the Persian Gulf area.

Invasion of Panama: Why Was the War Powers Issue Not Raised?

On December 20, 1989, President Bush ordered 14,000 U.S. military forces to Panama for combat, in addition to 13,000 already present. On December 21, he reported to Congress under the War Powers Resolution but without citing section 4(a)(1). His stated objectives were to protect the 35,000 American citizens in Panama, restore the democratic process, preserve the integrity of the Panama Canal treaties, and apprehend General Manuel Noriega, who had been accused of massive electoral fraud in the Panamanian elections and indicted on drug trafficking charges by two U.S. Federal courts. The operation proceeded swiftly and General Noriega surrendered to U.S. military authorities on January 3. President Bush said the objectives had been met, and U.S. forces were gradually withdrawn. By February 13, all combat forces deployed for the invasion had been withdrawn, leavingthe strength just under the 13,597 forces stationed in Panama prior to the invasion.

The President did not consult with congressional leaders before his decision, although he did notify them a few hours in advance of the invasion. Members of Congress had been discussing the problem of General Noriega for some time. Before Congress adjourned, it had called for the President to intensify unilateral, bilateral, and multilateral measures and consult with other nations on ways to coordinate efforts to remove General Noriega from power.[49] The Senate had adopted an amendment supporting the President's use of appropriate diplomatic, economic, and military options "to restore constitutional government to Panama and to remove General Noriega from his illegal control of the Republic of Panama", but had defeated an amendment authorizing thePresident to use U.S. military force to secure the removal of General Noriega "notwithstanding any other provision of law."[50]

The Panama action did not raise much discussion in Congress about the War Powers Resolution. This was in part because Congress was out of session. The first session of the 101st Congress had ended on November 22, 1989, and the second session did not begin until January 23, 1990, when the operation was essentially over and it appeared likely the additional combat forces would be out of Panama within 60 days of their deployment. Moreover, the President's action in Panama was very popular in American public opinion and supported by most Members of Congress because of the actions of General Noriega. After it was over, on February 7, 1990, the House Passed H.Con.Res. 262 which stated that the President had acted "decisively and appropriately in ordering United States forces to intervene in Panama."

MAJOR CASES AND ISSUES IN THE POST-COLD WAR WORLD: UNITED NATIONS ACTIONS

After the end of the Cold War in 1990, the United States began to move away from unilateral military actions toward actions authorized or supported bythe United Nations. Under the auspices of U.N. Security Council resolutions, U.S. forces were deployed in Kuwait and Iraq, Somalia, former Yugoslavia/Bosnia/, and Haiti. This raised the new issue of whether the War Powers Resolution applied to U.S. participation in U.N. military actions. It was not a problem during the Cold War because the agreement among the five permanent members required for Security Council actions seldom existed. An exception, the Korean war, occurred before the War Powers Resolution was enacted.[51]

The more basic issue — under what circumstances congressional authorization is required for U.S. participation in U.N. military operations — is an unfinished debate remaining from 1945. Whether congressional authorization is required depends on the types of U.N. action and is governed by the U.N. Participation Act (P.L. 79-264, as amended), as well as by the War Powers Resolution and war powers under the Constitution. Appropriations action by Congress also may be determinative as a practical matter.

For armed actions under Articles 42 and 43 of the United Nations Charter, Section 6 of the U.N. Participation Act authorizes the President to negotiate special agreements with the Security Council "*which shall be subject to the approval of the Congress by appropriate Act or joint resolution*", providing for the numbers and types of armed forces and facilities to be made available to the Security Council. Once the agreements have been concluded, further congressional authorization is not necessary, but no such agreements have been concluded.

Section 7 of the United Nations Participation Act, added in 1949 by P.L. 81-341, authorizes the detail of up to 1,000 personnel to serve in any noncombatant capacity for certain U.N. peaceful settlement activities. The United States has provided personnel to several U.N. peacekeeping missions, such as observers to the U.N. Truce Supervision Organization in Palestine since 1948, that appear to fall within the authorization in Section 7 of the Participation Act. Controversy has arisen when larger numbers of forces have been deployed or when it appears the forces might be serving as combatants.

The War Powers Resolution neither excludes United Nations actions from its provisions nor makes any special procedures for them. Section 8(a)(2) states that authority to introduce U. S. Armed Forces into hostilities shall not be inferred from any treaty unless it is implemented by legislation specifically authorizing the introduction and stating that it is intended to constitute specific statutory authorization within the meaning of the War Powers resolution.[52] One purpose of this provision was to ensure that both Houses of Congress be affirmatively involved in anyU.S. decision to engage in hostilities pursuant to a treaty, since onlytheSenate approved a treaty. [53]

From 1990 through 1999, Congress primarily dealt with the issue on a case by case basis, but Members also enacted some measures seeking more control over U.S. participation in future peacekeepingactions wherever they might occur. The Defense Appropriations Act for FY1994 stated the sense of Congress that funds should not be expended for U.S. Armed Forces serving under U.N. Security Council actions unless the President consults with Congress at least 15 days prior to deployment and not later than 48 hours after such deployment, except for humanitarian operations.[54] The Defense Authorization Act for FY1994 required a report to Congress by April 1, 1994, including discussion of the requirement of congressional approval for participation of U.S. Armed Forces in multinational peacekeeping missions, proposals to conclude military agreements with the U.N. Security Council under Article 43 of the U.N. Charter, and the applicability of the War Powers Resolution and the U.N. Participation Act.[55] In 1994 and 1995, Congress attempted to gain a greater role in U.N. and other peacekeeping operations through authorization and appropriation legislation. A major element of the House Republicans' **Contract with America, H.R. 7, would** have placed notable constraints on Presidential authority to commit U.S. forces to **international peacekeeping operations. Senator Dole's, S. 5, The Peace Powers**

Act, introduced in January 1995, would have also placed greater legislative controls on such operations. General and specific funding restrictions and Presidential reporting requirements were passed for peacekeeping operations underway or in prospect. Some of these legislative enactments led to Presidential vetoes. These representative legislative actions are reviewed below as they apply to given cases.[56]

Persian Gulf War, 1991: How Does the War Powers Resolution Relate to the United Nations and a Real War?

On August 2, 1990, Iraqi troops under the direction of President Saddam Hussein invaded Kuwait, seized its oil fields, installed a new government in Kuwait City, and moved on toward the border with Saudi Arabia. Action to repel the invasion led to the largest war in which the United States has been involved since the passage of the War Powers Resolution. Throughout the effort to repel the Iraqi invasion, President Bush worked in tandem with the United Nations, organizing and obtaining international support and authorization for multilateral military action against Iraq.

A week after the invasion, on August 9, President Bush reported to Congress "consistent with theWar Powers Resolution" that he had deployed U.S. armed forces to the region prepared to take action with others to deter Iraqi aggression. He did not cite section 4(a)(1) and specifically stated, "I do not believe involvement in hostilities is imminent."

The President did not consult with congressional leaders prior to the deployment, but both houses of Congress had adopted legislation supporting efforts to end the Iraqi occupation of Kuwait, particularly using economic sanctions and multilateral efforts. On August 2, shortly before its recess, the Senate by a vote of 97-0 adopted S.Res. 318 urging the President "to act immediately, using unilateral and multilateral measures, to seek the full and unconditional withdrawal of all Iraqi forces from Kuwaiti territory" and to work for collective international sanctions against Iraq including, if economic sanctions prove inadequate, "additional multilateral actions, under Article 42 of the United Nations Charter, involving air, sea, and land forces as may be needed..." Senate Foreign Relations Committee Chairman Pell stressed, however, that the measure did not authorize unilateral U.S. military actions. Also on August 2, the House passed H.R. 5431 condemning the Iraqi invasion and calling for an economic embargo against Iraq.

The United Nations imposed economic sanctions against Iraq on August 7, and the United States and United Kingdom organized an international naval interdiction effort.[57] Later, on August 25, the U.N. Security Council authorized "such measures as may be necessary" to halt shipping and verify cargoes that might be going to Iraq.

Both Houses adopted measures supporting the deployment, but neither measure was enacted. On October 1, 1990, the House passed H.J.Res. 658 supporting the action and citing the War Powers Resolution without stating that Section 4(a)(1) had become operative. The resolution quoted the President's statement that involvement in hostilities was not imminent. Representative Fascell stated that H.J.Res. 658 was not to be interpreted as a Gulf of Tonkin resolution that granted the President open-ended authority, and that it made clear that "a congressional decision on the issue of war or peace would have to be made through joint consultation." The Senate did not act on H.J.Res. 658.

On October 2, 1990, the Senate by a vote of 96-3 adopted S.Con.Res. 147, stating that "Congress supports continued action by the President in accordance with the decisions of the United Nations Security Council and in accordance with United States constitutional and statutory processes, including the authorization and appropriation of funds by the Congress, to deter Iraqi aggression and to protect American lives and vital interest in the region." As in the House, Senate leaders emphasized that the resolution was not to be interpreted as an open-ended resolution similar to the Gulf of Tonkin resolution. The resolution made no mention of the War Powers Resolution. The House did not act on S.Con.Res. 147. Congress also supported the action by appropriating funds for the preparatory operation, called Operation Desert Shield, and later for war activities called Operation Desert Storm.

Some Members introduced legislation to establish a special consultation group, but the Administration objected to a formally established group. On October 23, 1990, Senate Majority Leader Mitchell announced that he and Speaker Foley had designated Members of the joint bipartisan leadership and committees of jurisdiction to make themselves available as a group for consultation on developments in the Persian Gulf. By this time U.S. land, naval, and air forces numbering more than 200,000 had been deployed.

After the 101st Congress had adjourned, President Bush on November 8, 1990, ordered an estimated additional 150,000 troops to the Gulf. He incurred considerable criticism because he had not informed the consultation group of the buildup although he had met with them on October 30. On November 16, President Bush sent a second report to Congress describing the continuing and increasing deployment of forces to the region. He stated that his opinion that hostilities were not imminent had not changed. The President wrote, "The deployment will ensure that the coalition has an adequate offensive military option should that be necessary to achieve our common goals." By the end of the year, approximately 350,000 U.S. forces had been deployed to the area.

As the prospect of a war without congressional authorization increased, on November 20, 1990, Representative Ron Dellums and 44 other Democratic Members of Congress sought a judicial order enjoining the President from offensive military operations in connection with Operation Desert Shield unless he consulted with and obtained an authorization from Congress. On November 26, 11 prominent law professors filed a brief in favor of such a judicial action, arguing that the Constitution clearly vested Congress with the authority to declare war and that Federal judges should not use the political questions doctrine to avoid ruling on the issue. The American Civil Liberties Union also filed a memorandum in favor of the plaintiffs. On December 13, Judge Harold Greene of the Federal district court in Washington denied the injunction, holding that the controversy was not ripe for judicial resolution because a majority of Congress had not sought relief and the executive branch had not shown sufficient commitment to a definitive course of action.[58] However, throughout his opinion Judge Greene rejected the Administration's arguments for full Presidential war powers.

On November 29, 1990, U.N. Security Council Resolution 678 authorized member states to use "all necessary means" to implement the Council's resolutions and restore peace and security in the area, unless Iraq complied with the U.N. resolutions by January 15, 1991. As the deadline for Iraqi withdrawal from Kuwait neared, President Bush indicated that if the Iraqi forces did not withdraw from Kuwait, he was prepared to use force to implement the U.N. Security Council resolutions. Administration officials contended that the President did not need any additional congressional authorization for this purpose.[59]

After the 102nd Congress convened, on January 4, 1991, House and Senate leaders announced they would debate U.S. policy beginning January 10. A week before the January 15 deadline, on January 8, 1991, President Bush, in a letter to the congressional leaders, requested a congressional resolution supporting the use of all necessary means to implement U.N. Security Council Resolution 678. He stated that he was "determined to do whatever is necessary to protect America's security" and that he could "think of no better way than for Congress to express its support for the President at this critical time." It is noteworthy that the President's request for a resolution was a request for congressional "support" for his undertaking in the Persian Gulf, not for "authority" to engage in the military operation. In a press conference on January 9, 1991, President Bush reinforced this distinction in response to questions about the use of force resolution being debated in Congress. He was asked whether he thought he needed the resolution, and if he lost on it would he feel bound by that decision. President Bush in response stated: "I don't think I need it...I feel that I have the authority to fully implement the United Nations resolutions." He added that he felt that he had "the constitutional authority — many attorneys having so advised me."[60]

On January 12, 1991, both houses passed the "Authorization for Use of Military Force Against Iraq Resolution" (P.L. 102-1).[61] Section 2(a) authorized the President to use U.S. Armed Forces pursuant to U.N. Security Council Resolution 678 to achieve implementation of the earlier Security Council resolutions. Section 2(b) required that first the President would have to report that the United States had used all appropriate diplomatic and other peaceful means to obtain compliance by Iraq with the Security Council resolution and that those efforts had not been successful. Section 2(c) stated that it was intended to constitute specific statutory authorization within the meaning of Section 5(b) of the War Powers Resolution. Section 3 required the President to report every 60 days on efforts to obtain compliance of Iraq with the U.N. Security Council resolution.

In his statement made after signing H.J.Res. 77 into law, President Bush said the following: "As I made clear to congressional leaders at the outset, my request for congressional support did not, and mysigning this resolution does not, constitute any change in the long-standing positions of the executive branch on either the President's constitutional authority to use the Armed Forces to defend vital U.S. interests or the constitutionality of the War Powers Resolution." He added that he was pleased that "differences on these issues between the President and many in the Congress have not prevented us from uniting in a common objective."[62]

On January 16, President Bush made the determination required by P.L. 102-1 that diplomatic means had not and would not compel Iraq to withdraw from Kuwait. On January 18, he reported to Congress "consistent with the War Powers Resolution" that he had directed U.S. forces to commence combat operations on January 16.

After the beginning of the war Members of Congress strongly supported the President as Commander-in-Chief in his conduct of the war. On March 19, 1991, President Bush reported to Congress that the military operations had been successful, Kuwait had been liberated, and combat operations had been suspended on February 28, 1991.

Prior to passage of P.L. 102-1, some observers questioned the effectiveness of the War Powers Resolution on grounds that the President had begun the action, deployed hundreds of thousands of troops without consultation of Congress, and was moving the Nation increasingly close to war without congressional authorization. After the passage of P.L. 102-1 and the war had begun, Chairman of the House Committee on Foreign Affairs Fascell took the position that "the War Powers Resolution is alive and well"; the President had submitted reports to Congress, and Congress, in P.L. 102-1, had provided specific statutory authorization for the use of force. In his view, the strength and wisdom of the War Powers Resolution was that it established a process by which Congress could authorize the use of force in specific settings for limited purposes, short of a total state of war.

The question is sometimes raised why Congress did not declare war against Iraq. Speaker Foley told the National Press Club on February 7, 1991, that "The reason we did not declare a formal war was not because there is any difference I think in the action that was taken and in a formal declaration of war with respect to military operations, but because there is some question about whether we wish to excite or enact some of the domestic consequences of a formal declaration of war — seizure of property, censorship, and so forth, which the President neither sought nor desired."

IRAQ-POST GULF WAR: HOW LONG DOES AN AUTHORIZATION LAST?

After the end of Operation Desert Storm, U.S. military forces were used to deal with three continuing situations in Iraq. These activities raised the issue of how long a congressional authorization for the use of force lasts.

The first situation resulted from the Iraqi government's repression of Kurdish and Shi'ite groups. U.N. Security Council Resolution 688 of April 5, 1991, condemned the repression of the Iraqi civilian population and appealed for contributions to humanitarian relief efforts. On May 17, 1991, President Bush reported to Congress that the Iraqi repression of the Kurdish people had necessitated a limited introduction of U.S. forces into northern Iraq for emergency relief purposes. On July 16, 1991, he reported that U.S. forces had withdrawn from northern Iraq but that the U.S. remained prepared to take appropriate steps as the situation required and that, to this end, an appropriate level of forces would be maintained in the region for "as long as required."

A second situation stemmed from the cease-fire resolution, Security Council Resolution 687 of April 3, 1991, which called for Iraq to accept the destruction or removal of chemical and biological weapons and international control of its nuclear materials. On September 16, 1991, President Bush reported to Congress that Iraq continued to deny inspection teams access to weapons facilities and that this violated the requirements of Resolution 687, and the United States if necessary would take action to ensure Iraqi compliance with the Council's decisions. He reported similar non-cooperation on January 14, 1992, and May 15, 1992.

On July 16, 1992, President Bush reported particular concern about the refusal of Iraqi authorities to grant U.N. inspectors access to the Agricultural Ministry. The President consulted congressional leaders on July 27, and in early August the United States began a series of military exercises to take 5,000 U.S. troops to Kuwait. On September 16, 1992, the President reported, "We will remain prepared to use all necessary means, in accordance with U.N. Security Council resolutions, to assist the United Nations in removing the threat posed by Iraq's chemical, biological, and nuclear weapons capability."

The third situation was related to both of the earlier ones. On August 26, 1992, the United States, Britain, and France began a "no-fly" zone, banning Iraqi fixed wing and helicopter flights south of the 32nd parallel and creating a limited security zone in the south, where Shi'ite groups were concentrated. After violations of the no-fly zones and various other actions by Iraq, on January 13, 1993, the Bush Administration announced that aircraft from the United States and coalition partners had attacked missile bases in southern Iraq and that the United States was deploying a battalion task force to Kuwait to underline the U.S. continuing commitment to Kuwait's independence. On January 19, 1993, President Bush reported to Congress that U.S. aircraft had shot down an Iraqi aircraft on December 27, 1992, and had undertaken further military actions on January 13, 17, and 18.

President Clinton said on January 21, 1993, that the United States would adhere to the policy toward Iraq set by the Bush Administration. On January 22 and 23, April 9 and 18, June 19, and August 19, 1993, U.S. aircraft fired at targets in Iraq after pilots sensed Iraqi radar or anti-aircraft fire directed at them. On September 23, 1993, President Clinton reported that since the August 19 action, the Iraqi installation fired upon had not displayed hostile intentions.

In a separate incident, on June 28, 1993, President Clinton reported to Congress "consistent with the War Powers Resolution"that on June 26 U.S. naval forces at his direction had launched a Tomahawk cruise missile strike on the Iraqi Intelligence Service's main command and control complex in Baghdad and that the military action was completed upon the impact of the missiles. He said the Iraqi Intelligence Service had planned the failed attempt to assassinate former President Bush during his visit to Kuwait in April 1993.

The question was raised as to whether the Authorization for the Use of Force in Iraq (P.L. 102-1) authorized military actions after the conclusion of the war. P.L. 102-1 authorized the President to use U.S. armed forces pursuant to U.N. Security Council Resolution 678 to achieve implementation of previous Security Council Resolutions relating to Iraq's invasion of Kuwait. The cease-fire resolution, Security Council Resolution 687, was adopted afterwards and therefore not included in Resolution 678.

Congress endorsed the view that further specific authorization was not required for U.S. military action to maintain the cease-fire agreement. Specifically, section 1095 of P.L.102-190 stated the sense of Congress that it supported the use of all necessary means to achieve the goals of Security Council Resolution 687 as being consistent with the Authorization for Use of Military Force Against Iraq Resolution. Section 1096 supported the use of all necessary means to protect Iraq's Kurdish minority, consistent with relevant U.N. resolutions and authorities contained in P.L. 102-1. The issue of Congressional authorization was debated again in 1998. On March 31, 1998, the House passed a Supplemental Appropriations bill (H.R. 3579) that would have banned the use of funds appropriated in it for the conduct of offensive operations against Iraq, unless such operations were specifically authorized by law. This provision was dropped in the conference with the Senate.

A more broad-gauged approach to the issue of Congressional authorization of military force was attempted in mid-1998. On June 24, 1998, the House passed H.R. 4103, the Defense Department Appropriations bill for FY1999, with a provision by Representative David Skaggs that banned the use of funds appropriated or otherwise made available by this Act "to initiate or conduct offensive military operations by United States Armed Forces except in accordance with the war powers clause of the Constitution (Article 1, Section 8), which vests in Congress the power to declare and authorize war and to take certain specified, related actions." The Skaggs provision was stricken by the House-Senate conference committee on H.R. 4103.

As events developed, beginning in late 1998, and continuing into the period prior to the U.S. military invasion of Iraq in March 2003, the United

War Powers Resolution: Presidential Compliance   61

States conducted a large number of ad-hoc air attacks against Iraqi ground installations and military targets in response to violations of the Northern and Southern "no-fly zones" by the Iraqi, and threatening actions taken against U.S. and coalition aircraft enforcing these "no-fly" sectors. Congressional authorization to continue these activities was not sought by the President, nor were these many incidents reported under the War Powers Resolution. The "no-fly zones" activities were terminated following the 2003 War with Iraq.

Somalia: When Does Humanitarian Assistance Require Congressional Authorization?

In Somalia, the participation of U.S. military forces in a U.N. operation to protect humanitarian assistance became increasingly controversial as fighting and casualties increased and the objectives of the operation appeared to be expanding.

On December 4, 1992, President Bush ordered thousands of U.S. militaryforces to Somalia to protect humanitarian relief from armed gangs. Earlier, on November 25, the President had offered U.S. forces, and on December 3, the United Nations Security Council had adopted Resolution 794 welcoming the U.S. offer and authorizing the Secretary-General and members cooperating in the U.S. offer "to use all necessary means to establish as soon as possible a secure environment for humanitarian relief operations in Somalia." The resolution also called on member states to provide military forces and authorized the Secretary-General and the states concerned to arrange for unified command and control.

On December 10, 1992, President Bush reported to Congress "consistent with the War Powers Resolution" that on December 8, U.S.armed forces entered Somalia to secure the air field and port facility of Mogadishu and that other elements of the U.S. armed forces were being introduced into Somalia to achieve the objectives of U.N. Security Council Resolution 794. He said the forces would remain only as long as necessary toestablish a secure environment for humanitarian relief operations and would then turn over responsibility for maintaining this environment to a U.N. peacekeeping force. The President said that it was not intended that the U.S. armed forces become involved in hostilities, but that the forces were equipped and ready to take such measures as might be needed to accomplish their humanitarian mission and defend themselves. They would also have the support of any additional U.S. forces necessary. By mid-January, U.S. forces in Somalia numbered 25,000.

Since the President did not cite Section 4(a)(1), the 60-day time limit was not necessarily triggered. By February, however, the U.S. force strength was being reduced, and it was announced the United States expected to turn over responsibility for protecting humanitarian relief shipments in Somalia to a U.N. force that would include U.S. troops. On March 26, 1993, the Security Council adopted Resolution 814 expanding the mandate of the U.N. force and bringing about a transition from a U.S.-led force to a U.N.-led force (UNOSOM II). By the middle of May, when the changeto U.N. control took place, the U.S. forces were down to approximately 4,000 troops, primarily logistics and communications support teams, but also a rapid deployment force of U.S. Marines stationed on Navy ships.

Violence within Somalia began to increase again. On June 5, 1993, attacks killed 23 Pakistani peacekeepers, and a Somali regional leader, General Aidid, was believed responsible. The next day the U.N. Security Council adopted Resolution 837 reaffirming the authority of UNOSOM II to take all necessary measures against those responsible for the armed attacks. On June 10, 1993, President Clinton **reported "consistent with the War Powers Resolution"** that the U.S. Quick Reaction Forcehad executed military strikes to assist UNOSOM II in quelling violence against it. On July 1, President Clinton submitted another report, not mentioning the War Powers Resolution, describing further air and ground military operations aimed at securing **General Aidid's compound and neutralizing military capabilities that had been** an obstacle to U.N. efforts to deliver humanitarian relief and promote national reconstruction.

From the beginning, a major issue for Congress was whether to authorize U.S. action in Somalia. On February4, 1993, the Senate had passed S.J.Res. 45 that would authorize the President to use U.S. armed forces pursuant to U.N. Security Council Resolution 794. S.J.Res. 45 stated it was intended to constitute the specific statutory authorization under Section 5(b) of the War Powers Resolution. On May 25, 1993, the House amended S.J.Res. 45 to authorize U.S. forces to remain for one year. S.J.Res. 45 was then sent to the Senate for its concurrence, but the Senate did not act on the measure.

As sporadic fighting resulted in the deaths of Somali and U.N. forces, including Americans, controversy over the operation intensified, and Congress took action through other legislative channels. In September 1993 the House and Senate adopted amendments to the Defense Authorization Act for FY1994 asking that the President consult with Congress on policy toward Somalia, and report the goals, objectives, and anticipated jurisdiction of the U.S. mission in Somalia by October 15, 1993; the amendments expressed the sense that the

President by November 15, 1993, should seek and receive congressional authorization for the continued deployment of U.S. forces to Somalia.[63] On October 7, the President consulted with congressional leaders from both parties for over two hours on Somalia policy. On October 13, President Clinton sent a 33-page report to Congress on his Somalia policy and its objectives.

Meanwhile, on October 7 President Clinton said that most U.S. forces would be withdrawn from Somalia by March 31, 1994. To ensure this, the Defense Department Appropriations Act for FY1994, cut off funds for U.S. military operations in Somalia after March 31, 1994, unless the President obtained further spending authority from Congress.[64] Congress approved the use of U.S. military forces in Somalia only for the protection of American military personnel and bases and for helping maintain the flow of relief aid by giving the U.N. forces security and logistical support; it required that U.S. combat forces in Somalia remain under the command and control of U.S. commanders under the ultimate direction of the President.

Earlier, some Members suggested that the U.S. forces in Somalia were clearly in a situation of hostilities or imminent hostilities, and that if Congress did not authorize the troops to remain, the forces should be withdrawn within 60 to 90 days. After a letter from House Foreign Affairs Committee Ranking Minority Member Benjamin Gilman and Senate Foreign Relations Committee Ranking Minority Member Jesse Helms, Assistant Secretary Wendy Sherman replied on July 21, 1993, that no previous Administrations had considered that intermittent military engagements, whether constituting hostilities, would necessitate the withdrawal of forces pursuant to Section 5(b); and the War Powers Resolution, in their view, was intended to apply to sustained hostilities. The State Department did not believe congressional authorization was necessary, although congressional support would be welcome. On August 4, 1993, Representative Gilman asserted that August 4 might be remembered as the daythe War Powers Resolution died because combat broke out in Somalia on June 5 and the President had not withdrawn U.S. forces and Congress had "decided to look the other way." On October 22, 1993, Representative Gilman introduced H.Con.Res. 170 directing the President pursuant to section 5(c) of the War Powers Resolution to withdraw U.S. forces from Somalia by January 31, 1994. The House adopted an amended version calling for withdrawal by March 31, 1994.[65] The Senate did not act on this non-binding measure.

However, the Defense Appropriations Act for FY1995 (P.L. 103-335, signed September 30, 1994) prohibited the use of funds for the continuous presence of U.S. forces in Somalia, except for the protection of U.S. personnel, after September 30, 1994. Subsequently, on November 4, 1994, the U.N. SecurityCouncil decided to end the U.N. mission in Somalia by March 31, 1995. On March 3, 1995, U.S. forces completed their assistance to United Nations forces evacuating Somalia.

Another war powers issue was the adequacy of consultation before the dispatch of forces. On December 4, 1992, President Bush had met with a number of congressional leaders to brief them on the troop deployment. In his December 10 report, President Bush stressed that he had taken into account the views expressed in H.Con.Res. 370, S.Con.Res. 132, and P.L. 102-274 on the urgent need for action in Somalia. However, none of these resolutions explicitly authorized U.S. military action.

Former Yugoslavia/Bosnia/Kosovo: What If No Consensus Exists?

Bosnia

The issue of war powers and U.S. participation in United Nations actions was also raised by efforts to halt fighting in the territory of former Yugoslavia, initially in Bosnia. Because some of the U.S. action has been taken within a NATO framework, action in Bosnia has also raised the issue of whether action under NATO is exempt from the requirements of the War Powers Resolution or its standard for the exercise of war powers under the Constitution. Article 11 of the North Atlantic Treaty states that its provisions are to be carried out by the parties "in accordance with their respective constitutional processes," inferring some role for Congress in the event of war. Section 8(a) of the War Powers Resolution states that authorityto introduce U.S. forces into hostilities is not to be inferred from anytreaty, ratified before or after 1973, unless implementing legislation specifically authorizes such introduction and says it is intended to constitute an authorization within the meaning of the War Powers Resolution. Section 8(b) states that nothing in the War Powers Resolution should be construed to require further authorization for U.S. participation in the headquarters operations of militarycommands established before 1973, such as NATO headquarters operations.

On August 13, 1992, the U.N. Security Council adopted Resolution 770 calling on nations to take "all measures necessary" to facilitate the delivery of humanitarian assistance to Sarajevo. Many in Congress had been advocating more assistance to the victims of the conflict. On August 11, 1992, the Senate

War Powers Resolution: Presidential Compliance 65

had passed S.Res. 330 urging the President to work for a U.N. Security Council resolution such as was adopted, but saying that no U.S. military personnel should be introduced into hostilities without clearly defined objectives. On the same day, the House passed H.Res. 554 urging the Security Council to authorize measures, including the use of force, to ensure humanitarian relief.

During 1993 the United States participated in airlifts into Sarajevo, naval monitoring of sanctions, and aerial enforcement of a "no-fly zone." On February 10, 1993, Secretary of State Warren Christopher announced that under President Clinton, the United States would try to convince the Serbs, Muslims, and Croats to pursue a diplomatic solution and that if an agreement was reached, U.S. forces, including ground forces, would help enforce the peace. On February 28, 1993, the United States began an airdrop of relief supplies aimed at civilian populations, mainly Muslims, surrounded by fighting in Bosnia.

On March 31, 1993, the U.N. Security Council authorized member states to take all necessary measures to enforce the ban on military flights over Bosnia, the "no-fly zone". NATO planes, including U.S. planes, began patrolling over Bosnia and Herzegovina on April 12, 1993, to enforce the Security Council ban, and the next day, President Clinton reported the U.S. participation "consistent with Section 4 of the War Powers Resolution."

Conflict continued, but the situation was complicated and opinion in Congress and among U.N. and NATO members was divided. President Clinton consulted with about two dozen congressional leaders on potential further action on April 27 and received a wide range of views. On May 2, the Administration began consultation with allies to build support for additional military action to enforce a cease-fire and Bosnian Serb compliance with a peace agreement, but a consensus on action was not reached.

On June 10, 1993, Secretary of State Christopher announced the United States would send 300 U.S. troops to join 700 Scandinavians in the U.N. peacekeeping force in Macedonia.[66] The mission was established under U.N. Security Council Resolution 795 (1992), which sought to prevent the war in Bosnia from spilling over to neighboring countries. President Clinton reported this action "consistent with Section 4 of the War Powers Resolution" on July 9, 1993. He identified U.S. troops as part of a peacekeepingforce, and directed in accordance with Section 7 of the U.N. Participation Act.

Planning for U.N. and NATO action to implement a prospective peace agreement included the possibility that the United States might supply 25,000 out of 50,000 NATO forces to enforce U.N. decisions. This possibility brought proposals to require congressional approval before the dispatch of further forces to Bosnia. On September 23, 1993, Senate Minority Leader Robert Dole said he intended to offer an amendment stating that no additional U.S. forces should be introduced into former Yugoslavia without advance approval from Congress. Assistant Secretary of State Stephen Oxman said on October 5 that the Clinton Administration would consult with Congress and not commit American troops to the implementation operation for a peace agreement without congressional support, and that the Administration would act consistent with the War Powers Resolution. Congress sought to assure this in Section 8146 of P.L. 103-139, the Defense Appropriation Act for FY1994, stating the sense of Congress that funds should not be available for U.S. forces to participate in new missions or operations to implement the peace settlement in Bosnia unless previously authorized by Congress. This provision was sponsored by the Senate by leaders Mitchell and Dole.

At the NATO summit conference in Brussels on January 11, 1994, leaders, including President Clinton, repeated an August threat to undertake air strikes on Serb positions to save Sarajevo and to consider other steps to end the conflict in Bosnia. On February 17, 1994, President Clinton reported **"consistent with" the War Powers Resolution** that the United States had expanded its participation in United Nations and NATO efforts to reach a peaceful solution in former Yugoslaviaand that 60 U.S. aircraft were available for participation in the authorized NATO missions. On March 1, 1994, he reported that on the previous day U.S. **planes patrolling the "no-fly zone"** under the North Atlantic Treaty Organization (NATO) shot down 4 Serbian Galeb planes. On April 12, 1994, the President reported that on April 10 and **11, following shelling of Gorazde, one of the "safe areas," and a decision by** U.N. and NATO leaders, U.S. planes bombedBosnian Serbian nationalist positions around Gorazde. On August 22, 1994, President Clinton similarly reported that on August 5, U.S. planes under NATO had strafed a Bosnian Serb gun position in an exclusion zone. On September 22, 1994, two British and one U.S. aircraft bombed a Serbian tank in retaliation for Serb attacks on U.N. peacekeepers near Sarajevo; and on November 21 more than 30 planes from the United States, Britain, France, and the Netherlands bombed the runway of a Serb airfield in Croatia.

As the conflict in Bosnia continued, leaders in Congress called for greater congressional involvement in decisions. Senator Dole introduced S. 2042, calling for the United States to end unilaterally its arms embargo, conducted in accordance with a U.N. Security Council Resolution, against Bosnia and Herzegovina. On May 10, 1994, Senate Majority Leader George Mitchell introduced an amendment to authorize and approve the President's decision to carry out NATO decisions to support and protect UNPROFOR forces around designated safe areas; to use airpower in the Sarajevo region; and to authorize air strikes against Serb weapons around certain safe areas if these areas were attacked. The Mitchell amendment favored lifting the arms embargo but not unilaterally; it also stated no U.S. ground combat troops should be deployed in Bosnia unless previously authorized by Congress. The Senate adopted both the Dole proposal, as an amendment, and the Mitchell amendment on May 12, 1994, by votes of 50-49. The less stringent Mitchell amendment passed on a straight partyline vote. Yet thirteen Democrats voted for the Dole amendment, indicating a sentiment in both parties to assist the Bosnians in defending themselves. The Senate then adopted S. 2042 as amended. The House did not act on the measure.

The Defense Authorization Act for FY1995 (P.L. 103-337, signed October 5, 1994) provided, in Section 1404, the sense of the Congress that if the Bosnian Serbs did not accept the Contact Group proposal by October 15, 1994, the President should introduce a U.N. Security Council resolution to end the arms embargo by December 1, 1994; if the Security Council had not acted by November 15, 1994, no funds could be used to enforce the embargo other than those required of all U.N. members under Security Council Resolution 713. That sequence of events occurred and the United States stopped enforcing the embargo. In addition, Section 8100 of the Defense Appropriations Act, FY1995 (P.L. 103-335, signed September 30, 1994), stated the sense of the Congress that funds made available by this law should not be available for the purposes of deploying U.S. armed forces to participate in implementation of a peace settlement in Bosnia unless previously authorized by Congress.

On May 24, 1995, President Clinton reported "consistent with the War Powers Resolution" that U.S. combat-equipped fighter aircraft and other aircraft continued to contribute to NATO's enforcement of the no-fly zone in airspace over Bosnia-Herzegovina. U.S. aircraft, he noted, are also available for close air support of U.N. forces in Croatia. Roughly 500 U.S. soldiers were still deployed in the former Yugoslav Republic of Macedonia as part of the U.N. Preventive Deployment Force (UNPREDEP). U.S. forces continue to support U.N. refugee and embargo operations in this region.

On September 1, 1995, President Clinton reported "consistent with the War Powers Resolution," that "U.S. combat and support aircraft" had been used beginning on August 29, 1995, in a series of NATO air strikes against Bosnian Serb Army (BSA) forces in Bosnia-Herzegovina that were threatening the U.N.-declared safe areas of Sarajevo, Tuzla, and Gorazde." He noted that during the first day of operations, "some 300 sorties were flown against 23 targets in the vicinity of Sarajevo, Tuzla, Gorazde, and Mostar."

On September 7, 1995 the House passed an amendment to the FY1996 Department of Defense Appropriations Bill (H.R. 2126), offered by Representative Mark Neumann (R-WI.) that prohibited the obligation or expenditure of funds provided by the bill for any operations beyond those already undertaken. However, in conference the provision was softened to a sense-of-the-Congress provision that said that President must consult with Congress before deploying U.S. forces to Bosnia. The conference report was rejected by the House over issues unrelated to Bosnia on September 29, 1995 by a vote of 151-267. The substitute conference report on H.R. 2126, which was subsequently passed and signed into law, did not include language on Bosnia, in part due to the President's earlier objections to any provision in the bill that might impinge on his powers as Commander-in-Chief. On September 29, the Senate passed by a vote of 94-2 a sense-of-the-Senate amendment to H.R. 2076, the FY1996 State, Commerce, Justice Appropriations bill, sponsored by Senator Judd Gregg (R-N.H.) that said no funds in the bill should be used for the deployment of U.S. combat troops to Bosnia-Herzegovina unless Congress approves the deployment in advance or to evacuate endangered U.N. peacekeepers. The conference report on H.R. 2076, agreed to by the House and the Senate, included the "sense of the Senate" language of the Gregg amendment.

In response to mounting criticism of the Administration's approach to Bosnian policy,on October 17-18, 1995, Secretary of State Christopher, Secretary of Defense Perry and Joint Chiefs of Staff Chairman Shalikashvili testified before House and Senate Committeeson Bosniapolicyand the prospect of President Clinton deploying approximately 20,000 American ground forces as part of a NATO peacekeeping operation. During testimony before the Senate Foreign Relations Committee on October 17, Secretary Christopher stated that the President would not be bound by a resolution of the Congress prohibiting sending of U.S. forces into Bosnia without the express prior approval of Congress. Nevertheless, on October 19, 1995, President Clinton in a letter to Senator Robert C. Byrd stated that "[w]hile maintaining the constitutional authorities of the Presidency, I would welcome, encourage and, at the appropriate time, request an expression of support by the Congress" for the commitment of U.S. troops to a NATO implementation force in Bosnia, after a peace agreement is reached.

Subsequently, on October 30, 1995, the House, by a vote of 315-103, passed H.Res. 247, expressing the sense of the House that "no United States

Armed forces should be deployed on the ground in the territory of the Republic of Bosnia and Herzegovina to enforce a peace agreement until the Congress has approved such a deployment." On November 13, President Clinton's 9-page letter to Speaker Gingrich stated he would send a request "for a congressional expression of support for U.S. participation in a NATO-led Implementation Force in Bosnia ... before American forces are deployed in Bosnia." The President said there would be a "timely opportunity for Congress to consider and act upon" his request for support. He added that despite his desire for congressional support, he "must reserve" his "constitutional prerogatives in this area." On November 17, 1995, the House passed (243-171) H.R. 2606, which would "prohibit the use of funds appropriated or otherwise available" to the Defense Department from "being used for the deployment on the ground of United States Armed Forcesin the Republic of Bosnia-Herzegovina as part of any peacekeeping operation or as part of any implementation force, unless funds for such deployment are specifically appropriated" by law.

On December 4, 1995, Secretary of Defense Perry announced the deployment of about 1,400 U.S. military personnel (700 to Bosnia/700 to Croatia) as part of the advance elements of the roughly 60,000 person NATO Implementation Force in Bosnia, scheduled to deploy in force once the Dayton Peace Agreement is signed in Paris on December 14, 1995. Secretary Perry noted that once the NATO I-Force was fully deployed, about 20,000 U.S. military personnel would be in Bosnia, and about 5,000 in Croatia.

On December 6, 1995, President Clinton notified the Congress, "consistent with the War Powers Resolution," that he had "ordered the deployment of approximately 1,500 U.S. military personnel to Bosnia and Herzegovina and Croatia as part of a NATO 'enabling force' to lay the groundwork for the prompt and safe deployment of the NATO-led Implementation Force (IFOR)," which would be used to implement the Bosnian peace agreement after its signing. The President also noted that he had authorized deployment of roughly 3,000 other U.S. military personnel to Hungary, Italy, and Croatia to establish infrastructure for the enabling force and the IFOR.

In response to these developments, Congress addressed the question of U.S. ground troop deployments in Bosnia. Lawmakers sought to take action before the final Bosnian peace agreement was signed in Paris on December 14, 1995, following which the bulk of American military forces would be deployed to Bosnia. On December 13, 1995, the House considered H.R. 2770, sponsored by Representative Dornan, which would have prohibited the use of

Federal funds for the deployment "on the ground" of U.S. Armed Forces in Bosnia-Herzegovina "as part of any peacekeeping operation, or as part of any implementation force." H.R. 2770 was defeated in the House by a vote of 210-218. On December 13, the House considered two other measures. It approved H.Res. 302, offered by Representative Buyer, by a vote of 287-141. H.Res. 302, anon-binding measure, reiterated "serious concerns and opposition" to the deployment of U.S. ground troops to Bosnia, while expressing confidence, "pride and admiration" for U.S. soldiers deployed there. It called on the President and Defense Secretary to rely on the judgement of the U.S. ground commander in Bosnia and stated that he should be provided with sufficient resources to ensure the safety and well-being of U.S. troops. H.Res. 302, further stated that the U.S. government should "in all respects" be "impartial and evenhanded" with all parties to the Bosnian conflict "as necessary to ensure the safety and protection" of American forces in the region.

Subsequently, the House defeated H.Res 306, proposed by Representative Hamilton, by a vote of 190-237. H.Res 306 stated that the House "unequivocally supports the men and women of the United States Armed Forces who are carrying out their mission in support of peace in Bosnia and Herzegovina with professional excellence, dedicated patriotism and exemplary bravery."

On December 13, the Senate also considered three measures related to Bosnia and U.S. troop deployments. The Senate defeated H.R. 2606 by a vote of 22-77. This bill would have prohibited funds to be obligated or expended for U.S. participation in peacekeeping in Bosnia unless such funds were specifically appropriated for that purpose. The Senate also defeated S.Con.Res. 35, a non-binding resolution of Senators Hutchison and Inhofe. This resolution stated that "Congress opposes President Clinton's decision to deploy" U.S. troops to Bosnia, but noted that "Congress strongly supports" the U.S. troops sent by the President to Bosnia.

The Senate did pass S.J.Res. 44, sponsored by Senators Dole and McCain, by a vote of 69-30. This resolution stated that Congress "unequivocally supports the men and women of our Armed Forces" who were to be deployed to Bosnia. S.J.Res. 44 stated that "notwithstanding reservations expressed about President Clinton's decision" to deploy U.S. forces, "the President may only fulfill his commitment" to deploy them to Bosnia "for approximately one year" if he made a determination to Congress that the mission of the NATO peace implementation force (IFOR) will be limited to implementing the military annex to the Bosnian peace agreement and to protectingitself. The Presidential determination must also state that the United States will "lead an immediate international effort," separate from IFOR, "to provide equipment, arms, training and related logistics assistance of the highest possible quality" to the Muslim-Croat Federation so that it may provide for its own defense. The President could use"existing military drawdown authorities and requesting such additional authority as may be necessary." S.J.Res. 44 also required President Clinton to submit to Congress a detailed report on the armament effort within 30 days, and required regular Presidential reports to Congress on the implementation of both the military and non-military aspects of the peace accords.

The House and Senate did not appoint and direct conferees to meet to reconcile the conflicting elements of the Bosnia related measures each had passed on December 13, 1995. A number of Members and Senators had wished to express their views on the troop deployment before the Dayton Accords were formally signed in Paris. That action had occurred, and the leadership of both parties apparently believed nothing further would be achieved by a conference on the measures passed. As result, no final consensus on a single specific measure was reached on the issue by the two chambers.

The President meanwhile continued with the Bosnian deployment. On December 21, 1995, President Clinton notified Congress "consistent with the War Powers Resolution," that he had ordered the deployment of approximately 20,000 U.S. military personnel to participate in the NATO-led Implementation Force (IFOR) in the Republic of Bosnia-Herzegovina, and approximately 5,000 U.S. military personnel would be deployed in other former Yugoslav states, primarily in Croatia. In addition, about 7,000 U.S. support forces would be deployed to Hungary, Italy, Croatia, and other regional states in support of IFOR's mission. The President ordered participation of U.S. forces "pursuant to" his "constitutional authority to conduct the foreign relations of the United States and as Commander-in-Chief and Chief Executive."[67] Subsequently, President Clinton in December 1996, agreed to provide up to 8,500 ground troops to participate in a NATO-led follow-on force in Bosnia termed the Stabilization Force (SFOR). On March 18, 1998, the House defeated by a vote of 193-225, H.Con.Res. 227, a resolution of Representative Tom Campbell, directing the President, pursuant to section 5(c) of the War Powers Resolution to remove United States Armed Forces from the Republic of Bosnia and Herzegovina.(H.Rept. 105-442).[68]

Kosovo

The issue of Presidential authority to deploy forces in the absence of congressional authorization, under the War Powers Resolution, or otherwise, became an issue of renewed controversy in late March 1999 when President Clinton ordered U.S. military forces to participate in a NATO-led military operation in Kosovo. This action was the focus of a major policy debate over the purpose and scope of U.S. military involvement in Kosovo. The President's action to commit forces to the NATO Kosovo operation also led to a suit in Federal District Court for the District of Columbia by Members of Congress seeking a judicial finding that the President was violating the War Powers Resolution and the Constitution by using military forces in Yugoslavia in the absence of authorization from the Congress.

The Kosovo controversy began in earnest when on March 26, 1999, President Clinton notified the Congress "consistent with the War Powers Resolution", that on March 24, 1999, U.S. military forces, at his direction and in coalition with NATO allies, had commenced air strikes against Yugoslavia in response to the Yugoslav government's campaign of violence and repression against the ethnic Albanian population in Kosovo. Prior to the President's action, the Senate, on March 23, 1999, had passed, by a vote of 58-41, S.Con.Res. 21, a non-binding resolution expressing the sense of the Congress that the President was authorized to conduct "military air operations and missile strikes in cooperation with our NATO allies against the Federal Republic of Yugoslavia (Serbia and Montenegro)."

Subsequently, the House voted on a number of measures relating to U.S. participation in the NATO operation in Kosovo. On April 28, 1999, the House of Representatives passed H.R. 1569, by a vote of 249-180. This bill would prohibit the use of funds appropriated to the Defense Department from being used for the deployment of "ground elements" of the U.S. Armed Forces in the Federal Republic of Yugoslavia unless that deployment is specifically authorized by law. On that same day the House defeated H.Con.Res. 82, by a vote of 139-290. This resolution would have directed the President, pursuant to section 5(c) of the War Powers Resolution, to remove U.S. Armed Forces from their positions in connection with the present operations against the Federal Republic of Yugoslavia. On April 28, 1999, the House also defeated H.J.Res. 44, by a vote of 2-427. This joint resolution would have declared a state of war between the United States and the "Government of the Federal Republic of Yugoslavia." The House on that same day also defeated, on a 213-213 tie vote, S.Con.Res. 21, the Senate resolution passed on March 23, 1999, that supported military air operations and missile strikes against Yugoslavia.

On April 30, 1999, Representative Tom Campbell and 17 other members of the House filed suit in Federal District Court for the District of Columbia seeking a ruling requiring the President to obtain authorization from Congress before continuing the air war, or taking other military action against Yugoslavia.[69]

The Senate, on May 4, 1999, by a vote of 78-22, tabled S.J.Res. 20, a joint resolution, sponsored by Senator John McCain, that would authorize the President "to use all necessary force and other means, in concert with United States allies, to accomplish United States and North Atlantic Treaty Organization objectives in the Federal Republic of Yugoslavia (Serbia and Montenegro)."[70] The House, meanwhile, on May 6, 1999, by a vote of 117-301, defeated an amendment by Representative Ernest Istook to H.R. 1664, the FY1999 defense supplemental appropriations bill, that would have prohibited the expenditure of funds in the bill to implement any plan to use U.S. ground forces to invade Yugoslavia, except in time of war. Congress, meanwhile, on May 20, 1999 cleared for the President's signature, H.R. 1141, an emergency supplemental appropriations bill for FY1999, that provided billions in funding for the existing U.S. Kosovo operation.

The Senate tabled two other amendments that would have restricted military operations by President Clinton in Kosovo. On May 24, 1999, it tabled, by a vote of 52-48, an amendment offered by Senator Arlen Specter to state that no funds available to the Defense Department may be obligated or expended for the deployment of U.S. ground troops to Yugoslavia unless authorized by a declaration of war or a joint resolution authorizing the use of military force. The Specter amendment did not apply to certain actions, such as rescuing U.S. military personnel or citizens.[71] On May 26, 1999 the Senate tabled an amendment, by a vote of 77-21, offered by Senator Bob Smith to prohibit, effective October 1, 1999, the use of funds for militaryoperations in Yugoslavia unless Congress enacted specific authorization in law for the conduct of these operations.[72]

On May 25, 1999, the 60th day had passed since the President notified Congress of his actions regarding U.S. participation in military operations in Kosovo. Representative Campbell, and those who joined his suit, noted to the Federal Court that this was a clear violation of the language of the War Powers Resolution stipulating a withdrawal of U.S. forcesfrom theareaof hostilities after 60 days in the absence of congressional authorization to continue, or a Presidential request to Congress for an extra 30 day period to safely withdraw. The President did not seek such a 30 day extension, noting instead his view that the War Powers Resolution is constitutionally defective.

On June 8, 1999, Federal District Judge Paul L. Friedman dismissed the suit of Representative Campbell and others that sought to have the court rule that President Clinton was in violation of the War Powers Resolution and the Constitution by conducting military activities in Yugoslavia without having received prior authorization from Congress. The judge ruled that Representative Campbell and the other Congressional plaintiffs lacked legal standing to bring the suit.[73] On June 24, 1999, Representative Campbell appealed the ruling to the U.S. Court of Appeals for the District of Columbia. The appeals court subsequently agreed to hear the case on an expedited basis before Judges Silberman, Randolph, and Tatel. On February 18, 2000, the appeals court affirmed the opinion ofthe District Court that Representative Campbell and his co-plaintiffs lacked standing to sue the President.[74] On May 18, 2000, Representative Campbell and 30 other Members of Congress appealed this decision to the United States Supreme Court. On October 2, 2000, the United States Supreme Court, without comment, refused to hear the appeal of Representative Campbell, thereby letting stand the holding of the U.S. Court of Appeals.[75]

While Representative Campbell's litigation was continuing, Yugoslavia, on June 10, 1999, agreed to NATO conditions for a cease-fire and withdrawal of Yugoslav military and paramilitary personnel from Kosovo, and the creation of a peacekeeping force (KFOR) which had the sanction of the United Nations. Further, on June 10, 1999, the House of Representatives defeated, by a vote of 328-97, an amendment to H.R. 1401, the National Defense Authorization Act for FY2000-FY2001, that would have prohibited the use of any Defense Department funding in FY2000 for "military operations in the Federal Republic of Yugoslavia." On that same day, the House approved, by a vote of 270-155, an amendment that deleted, from the House reported version of H.R. 1401, language that would have prohibited any funding for "combat or peacekeeping operations" in the Federal Republic of Yugoslavia.

On June 12, 1999, President Clinton announced and reported to Congress "consistent with the War Powers Resolution" that he had directed the deployment of about "7,000 U.S. military personnel as the U.S. contribution to the approximately 50,000-member, NATO-led security force (KFOR)" currently being assembled in Kosovo. He also noted that about "1,500 U.S. military personnel, under separate U.S. command and control, will deploy to other countries in the region, as our national support element, in support of KFOR." Thus, by the summer of 1999, the President had been able to proceed with his policy of intervention in the Kosovo crisis under the aegis of NATO, the Congress had not achieved any position of consensus on what actions were

War Powers Resolution: Presidential Compliance   75

appropriate in Yugoslavia, and a U.S. District Court had dismissed a congressional lawsuit (a position subsequently affirmed the followingyear by the Appeals Court, and the U.S. Supreme Court) attemptingto stop Presidential military action in Yugoslavia in the absence of prior congressional authorization under the War Powers Resolution.[76]

Haiti: Can the President Order Enforcement of a U.N. Embargo?

On July 3, 1993, Haitian military leader Raoul Cedras and deposed President Jean-Bertrand Aristide signed an agreement providing for the restoration of President Aristide on October 30. The United Nations and Organization of American States took responsibility for verifying compliance. In conjunction with the agreement, President Clinton offered to send 350 troops and military engineers to Haiti to help retrain the Haitian armed forces and work on construction projects. A first group of American and Canadian troops arrived on October 6. When additional U.S. forces arrived on October 11, a group of armed civilians appeared intent upon resistingtheir landing, and on October 12 defense officials ordered the ship carrying them, the *U.S.S. Harlan County*, to leave Haitian waters.

Because the Haitian authorities were not complying with the agreement, on October 13 the U.N. Security Council voted to restore sanctions against Haiti. On October 20, President Clinton **reported "consistent with the War Powers Resolution" that U.S. ships had begun to enforce the U.N. embargo.** Some Members of Congress complained that Congress had not been consulted on or authorized the action. On October 18, Senator Dole said he would offer an amendment to the Defense Appropriations bill (H.R. 3116)which would require congressional authorization for all deployments into Haitian waters and airspace unless the President made specified certifications. Congressional leaders and Administration officials negotiated on the terms of the amendment. As enacted, section 8147 of P.L. 103-139 stated the sense of Congress that funds should not be obligated or expended for U.S. military operations in Haiti unless the operations were (1) authorizedin advance by Congress, (2) necessary to protect or evacuate U.S. citizens, (3) vital to the national security of the United States and there was not sufficient time to receive congressional authorization, or (4) the President reported in advance that the intended deployment met certain criteria.

Enforcement of the embargo intensified. On April 20, 1994, President Clinton further reported "consistent with the War Powers Resolution" that U.S. naval forces had continued enforcement in the waters around Haiti and that 712 vessels had been boarded. On May 6, 1994, the U.N. Security Council adopted Resolution 917 calling for measures to tighten the embargo. On June 10, 1994, President Clinton announced steps being taken to intensify the pressure on Haiti's military leaders that included assisting the Dominican Republic to seal its border with Haiti, using U.S. naval patrol boats to detain ships suspectedof violating the sanctions, a ban on commercial air traffic, and sanctions on financial transactions.

As conditions in Haiti worsened, President Clinton stated he would not rule out the use of force, and gradually this option appeared more certain. Many Members continued to contend congressional authorization was necessary for any invasion of Haiti. On May 24, 1994, the House adopted the Goss amendment to the Defense Authorization bill (H.R. 4301) by a vote of 223-201. The amendment expressed the sense of Congress that the United States should not undertake any military action against the mainland of Haiti unless the President first certified to Congress thatclear and present danger to U.S. citizens or interests required such action. Subsequently, on June 9 the House voted on the Goss amendment again. This time the House reversed itself and rejected the amendment by a vote of 195-226. On June 27, a point of order was sustained against an amendment to the State Department appropriations bill that sought to prohibit use of funds for any U.N. peacekeeping operation related to Haiti. On June 29, 1994, the Senate in action on H.R. 4226 repassed a provision identical to Section 8147 of P.L. 103-139 but rejected a measure making advance congressional authorization a binding requirement. On August 5 it tabled (rejected) by a vote of 31 to 63 an amendment to H.R. 4606 by Senator Specter prohibiting the President from using U.S. armed forces to depose the military leadership unless authorized in advance by Congress, necessary to protect U.S. citizens, or vital to U.S. interests.

President Clinton sought and obtained U.N. Security Council authorization for an invasion. On July 31, the U.N. Security Council authorized a multinational force to use "all necessary means to facilitate the departure from Haiti of the military leadership ... on the understanding that the cost of implementing this temporary operation will be borne by the participating Member States" (Resolution 940, 1994).

On August 3, the Senate adopted an amendment to the Department of Veterans Affairs appropriation, H.R. 4624, by a vote of 100-0 expressing its sense that the Security Council Resolution did not constitute authorization for the deployment of U.S. forces in Haiti under the Constitution or the War Powers Resolution. The amendment, however, was rejected in conference. President Clinton said the same day that he would welcome the support of Congress but did not agree that he was constitutionally mandated to obtain it. Some Members introduced resolutions, such as H.Con.Res. 276, calling for congressional authorization prior to the invasion.

On September 15, 1994, in an address to the Nation, President Clinton said he had called up the military reserve and ordered two aircraft carriers into the region. His message to the military dictators was to leave now or the United States would force them from power. The first phase of military action would remove the dictators from power and restore Haiti's democratically elected government. The second phase would involve a much smaller force joining with forces from other U.N. members which would leave Haiti after 1995 elections were held and a new government installed.

While the Defense Department continued to prepare for an invasion within days, on September 16 President Clinton sent to Haiti a negotiating team of former President Jimmy Carter, former Joint Chiefs of Staff Chairman Colin Powell, and Senate Armed Services Committee Chairman Sam Nunn. Again addressing the Nation on September 18, President Clinton announced that the military leaders had agreed to step down by October 15, and agreed to the immediate introduction of troops, beginning September 19, from the 15,000 member international coalition. He said the agreement was only possible because of the credible and imminent threat of multinational force. He emphasized the mission still had risks and there remained possibilities of violence directed at U.S. troops, but the agreement minimized those risks. He also said that under U.N. Security Council resolution 940, a 25-nation international coalition would soon go to Haiti to begin the task of restoring democratic government. Also on September 18, President Clinton reported to Congress on the objectives in accordance with the sense expressed in Section 8147 (c) of P.L. 103-139, the FY1994 Defense Appropriations Act.

U.S. forces entered Haiti on September 1994. On September 21, President Clinton reported "consistent with the War Powers Resolution" the deployment of 1,500 troops, to be increased by several thousand. (At the peak in September there were about 21,000 U.S. forces in Haiti.) He said the U.S. presence would not be open-ended but would be replaced after a period of months by a U.N. peacekeeping force, although some U.S. forces would participate in and be present for the duration of the U.N. mission. The forces were involved in the first hostilities on September 24 when U.S. Marines killed 10 armed Haitian resisters in a fire-fight.

On September 19, the House agreed to H.Con.Res. 290 commending the President and the special delegation to Haiti, and supporting the prompt and orderly withdrawal of U.S. forces from Haiti as soon as possible; on September 19, the Senate agreed to a similar measure, S.Res. 259. On October 3, 1994, the House Foreign Affairs Committee reported H.J.Res. 416 authorizing the forces in Haiti until March 1, 1995, and providing procedures for a joint resolution to withdraw the forces. In House debate on October 6 the House voted against the original contents and for the Dellums substitute. As passed, H.J.Res. 416 stated the sense that the President should have sought congressional approval before deploying U.S. forces to Haiti, supporting a prompt and orderly withdrawal as soon as possible, and requiring a monthly report on Haiti as well as other reports. This same language was also adopted by the Senate on October 6 as S.J.Res. 229, and on October 7 the House passed S.J.Res. 229. President Clinton signed S.J.Res. 229 on October 25, 1994 (P.L. 103-423).

After U.S. forces began to disarm Haitian military and paramilitary forces and President Aristide returned on October 15, 1994, the United States began to withdraw some forces. On March 31, 1995, U.N. peacekeeping forces assumed responsibility for missions previously conducted by U.S. military forces in Haiti. By September 21, 1995, President Clinton reported the United States had 2,400 military personnel in Haiti as participants in the U.N. Mission in Haiti (UNMIH), and 260 U.S. military personnel assigned to the U.S. Support Group Haiti. On February 29, 1996, the U.S. Commander of the UNMIH was replaced and U.S. forces ceased to conduct security operations in Haiti, except for self defense. The majority of the 1,907 U.S. military personnel in Haiti were withdrawn by mid-March 1996, and the remainder, who stayed to arrange the dismantlement and repatriation of equipment, were withdrawn in mid-April 1996. After that, a U.S. support unit of 300 to 500 troops, made up primarily of engineers, remained in Haiti carrying out public works such as building bridges, repairing schools, and digging wells. In December 1997, President Clinton ordered the Dept. of Defense to maintain hundreds of U.S. troops in Haiti indefinitely. In September 1999, however, the 106th Congress passed the FY2000 DOD authorization bill (P.L. 106-65) that prohibited DOD funding to maintain a continuous U.S. military presence in Haiti beyond May 31, 2000. The troops were withdrawn by the end of January 2000. According to the conference report accompanying the FY2000 DOD

War Powers Resolution: Presidential Compliance   79

authorization bill (H.Rept. 106-301), the President is not prohibited from engaging in periodic theater engagement activities in Haiti.[77]

Terrorist Attacks against the United States (World Trade Center and the Pentagon) 2001: How Does the War Powers Resolution Apply?

On September 11, 2001, terrorists hijacked four U.S. commercial airliners, crashing two into the twin towers of the World Trade Center in New York City, and another into the Pentagon building in Arlington, Virginia. The fourth plane crashed in Shanksville, Pennsylvania near Pittsburgh, after passengers struggled with the highjackers for control of the aircraft. The death toll from these incidents was more than three thousand, making the attacks the most devastating of their kind in United States history. President George W. Bush characterized these attacks as more than acts of terror. "They were acts of war," he said. He added that "freedom and democracy are under attack," and he asserted that the United States would use "all of our resources to conquer this enemy."[78]

In the days immediately after the September 11 attacks, the President consulted with the leaders of Congress on appropriate steps to take to deal with the situation confronting the United States. One of the things that emerged from discussions with the White House and congressional leaders was the concept of a joint resolution of the Congress authorizing the President to take military steps to deal with the parties responsible for the attacks on the United States. Between September 13 and 14, draft language of such a resolution was discussed and negotiated by the President's representatives and the House and Senate leadership of both parties. Other members of both Houses suggested language for consideration. On Friday, September 14, 2001, the text of a joint resolution was introduced. It was first considered and passed by the Senate in the morning of September 14, as Senate Joint Resolution 23, by a vote of 98-0. The House of Representatives passed it later that evening, by a vote of 420-1, after tabling an identical resolution, H.J.Res. 64, and rejecting a motion to recommit by Representative John Tierney that would have had the effect, if passed and enacted, of requiring a report from the President on his actions under the resolution every 60 days.[79]

Senate Joint Resolution 23, titled the "Authorization for Use of Military Force," passed by Congress on September 14, 2001, was signed into law on September 18, 2001.[80] The joint resolution authorizes the President

> to use all necessary and appropriate force against those nations, organizations, or persons he determines planned, authorized, committed, or aided the terrorist attacks that occurred on September 11, 2001, or harbored such organizations or persons, in order to prevent any future acts of international terrorism against the United States by such nations, organizations or persons.

The joint resolution further states that Congress declares that this resolution is intended to "constitute specific statutory authorization within the meaning of section 5(b) of the War Powers Resolution." Finally, the joint resolution also states that "[n]othing in this resolution supercedes any requirement of the War Powers Resolution."

A notable feature of S.J.Res. 23 is that unlike all other major legislation authorizing the use of military force by the President, this joint resolution authorizes military force against "organizations and persons" linked to the September 11, 2001 attacks on the United States. Past authorizations of the use of force have permitted action against unnamed nations in specific regions of the world or against named individual nations. This authorization of military action against "organizations or persons" is unprecedented in American history, with the scope of its reach yet to be determined. The authorization of use of force against unnamed nations is more consistent with some previous instances where authority was given to act against unnamed states as appropriate when they became aggressors or took military action against the United States or its citizens.[81]

President George W. Bush in signing S.J.Res. on September 18, 2001, noted the Congress had acted "wisely, decisively, and in the finest traditions of our country." He thanked the "leadership of both Houses for their role in expeditiouslypassingthis historic joint resolution." He noted that he had had the "benefit of meaningful consultations with members of the Congress" since the September 11 attacks and that he would "continue to consult closely with them as our Nation responds to this threat to our peace and security." President Bush also asserted that S.J.Res. 23 "recognized the authority of the President under the Constitution to take action to deter and prevent acts of terrorism against the United States." He also stated: "In signing this resolution, I maintain the longstandingposition of the executive branch regarding the

War Powers Resolution: Presidential Compliance 81

President's constitutional authority to use force, including the Armed Forces of the United States and regarding the constitutionality of the War Powers Resolution."[82]

Prior to its enactment, there was concern among some in Congress that the President might not adhere to the reporting requirements of the War Powers Resolution when he exercised the authority provided in S.J.Res. 23. There appeared to be general agreement that the President had committed himself to consult with the Congress on matters related to his military actions against terrorists and those associated with the attacks on the United States on September 11. On September 24, 2001, President Bush reported to Congress, "consistent with the War Powers Resolution," and "Senate Joint Resolution 23" that in response to terrorist attacks on the World Trade Center and the Pentagon he had ordered the "deployment of various combat-equipped and combat support forces to a number of foreign nations in the Central and Pacific Command areas of operations." The President noted that as part of efforts to "prevent and deter terrorism" he might find it necessary to order additional forces into these and other areas of the world...." He stated that he could not now predict "the scope and duration of these deployments," nor the "actions necessary to counter the terrorist threat to the United States."

Subsequently, on October 9, 2001, President George W. Bush reported to Congress, "consistent with the War Powers Resolution," and "Senate Joint Resolution 23" that on October 7, 2001, U.S. Armed Forces "began combat action in Afghanistan against Al Qaida terrorists and their Taliban supporters." The President stated that he had directed thismilitaryaction in response to the September 11, 2001 attacks on U.S. "territory, our citizens, and our way of life, and to the continuing threat of terrorist acts against theUnited States and our friends and allies." This military action was "part of our campaign against terrorism" and was "designed to disrupt the use of Afghanistan as a terrorist base of operations."

Thus, in light of the September 11, 2001 terrorist attacks against United States territory and citizens, the President and the Congress, after consultations, agreed to a course of legislative action that did not invoke the War Powers Resolution itself, but substituted a specific authorization measure, S.J.Res. 23. Pursuit of such an action is contemplated by the language of the War Powers Resolution itself. As of the end of October 2001, President Bush had chosen to state in his reports to Congress that the military actions he had taken relating to the terrorists attacks were "consistent with" both the War Powers Resolution and Senate Joint Resolution 23. His actions follow the practiceof his White House predecessors in not formally citing the language of the War Powers Resolution in section 4(a)(1) that would trigger a military forces withdrawal timetable. Congress for its part in S. J. Res. 23 stated that this legislation constituted "specific statutory authorization within the meaning of section 5(b) of the War Powers Resolution." It also noted that "nothing" in S.J.Res. 23 "supercedes any requirement of the War Powers Resolution." The President and the Congress, in sum, maintained their respective positions on the constitutionality of the War Powers Resolution and the responsibilities of the President under it, while finding a legislative vehicle around which both branches could unite to support the President's response to the terrorist attacks on the United States.

Use of Force against Iraq Resolution 2002: A Classic Application of the War Powers Resolution?

In the summer of 2002, the Bush Administration made public its views regarding what it deemed a significant threat to U.S. interests and security posed by the prospect that Iraq had or was acquiring weapons of mass destruction. Senior members of the Bush Administration cited a number of violations of U.N. Security Council resolutions by Iraq regarding the obligation imposed at the end of the Gulf War in 1991 to end its chemical, biological and nuclear weapons programs. On September 4, 2002, President Bush met with leaders from both Houses and parties at the White House. At that meeting the President stated that he would seek Congressional support, in the near future, for action deemed necessary to deal with the threat posed to the United States by the regime of Saddam Hussein of Iraq. The President also indicated that he would speak to the United Nations shortly and set out his concerns about Iraq.

On September 12, 2002, President Bush addressed the U.N. General Assembly and set out the history of Iraqi misdeeds over the last two decades and the numerous times that Iraq had not fulfilled its commitments to comply with various U.N. Security Council resolutions, including disarmament, since the Gulf War of 1991. He stated that the United States would work with the U.N. Security Council to deal with Iraq's challenge. However, he emphasized that if Iraq refused to fulfill its obligations to comply with U.N. Security Council resolutions, the United States would see that those resolutions were enforced.[83]

Subsequently, on September 19, 2002, the White House sent a "draft" joint resolution to House Speaker Dennis Hastert, House Minority Leader

Richard Gephardt, Senate Majority Leader Thomas Daschle and Senate Minority Leader Trent Lott. This draft would have authorized the President to use military force not only against Iraq but "to restore international peace and security in the region." Subsequently introduced as S.J.Res. 45 on September 26, it served as the basis for an extensive debate over the desirability, necessity, and scope of a new Congressional authorization for the use of force. The Senate used this bill as the focus for a debate which began, after cloture was invoked, on October 3. The Senate debate continued from October 4 until October 11, 2002, and involved consideration of numerous amendments to the measure. In the end the Senate adopted H.J.Res. 114 in lieu of S.J.Res. 45.

The draft measure was not formally introduced in the House. Instead, the vehicle for House consideration of the issue was H.J.Res. 114. Cosponsored by Speaker Hastert and Minority Leader Gephardt and introduced on October 2, 2002, H.J.Res. 114 embodied modifications to the White House draft that were agreeable to the White House, most House and Senate Republicans, and the House Democratic leader. The House International Relations Committee reported out a slightly amended version of the joint resolution on October 7, 2002 (H. Report 107-721). The House adopted the rule governing debate on the joint resolution (H.Res. 474) on October 8, 2002; and debated the measure until October 10, when it passed H.J.Res. 114 by a vote of 296-133. Subsequently, the Senate passed the House version of H.J. Res 144 on October 11 by a vote of 77-23, and President Bush signed the "Authorization for Use of Military Force against Iraq Resolution of 2002" into law on October 16, 2002. [84]

In signing H.J.Res. 114 into law, President Bush noted that by passing this legislation the Congress had demonstrated that "the United States speaks with one voice on the threat to international peace and security posed by Iraq." He added that the legislation carried an important message that "Iraq will either comply with all U.N. resolutions, rid itself of weapons of mass destruction, and ...its support for terrorists, or will be compelled to do so." While the President noted he had sought a "resolution of support" from Congress to use force against Iraq, and appreciated receiving that support, he also stated that:

> ...my request for it did not, and my signing this resolution does not, constitute any change in the long-standing positions of the executive branch on either the President's constitutional authority to use force to deter, prevent, or respond to aggression or other threats to U.S.interests or on the constitutionality of the War Powers Resolution.

The President went on to state that on the "important question of the threat posed by Iraq", his views and goals and those of the Congress were the same. He further observed that he had extensive consultations with the Congress in the past months, and that he looked forward to "continuing close consultation in the months ahead." He stated his intent to submit written reports to Congress every 60 days on matters "relevant to this resolution."[85]

The central element of P.L. 107-243 is the authorization for the President to use the armed forces of the United States

> as he determines to be necessary and appropriate in order to (1) defend the national security of the United States against the continuing threat posed byIraq; and (2) enforce all relevant United Nations Security Council resolutions regarding Iraq.

As predicates for the use of force, the statute requires the President to communicate to Congress his determination that the use of diplomatic and other peaceful means will not "adequately protect the United States ... or ... lead to enforcement of all relevant United Nations Security Council resolutions" and that the use of force is "consistent" with the battle against terrorism. Like P.L. 102-1 and P.L. 107-40, the statute declares that it is "intended to constitute specific statutory authorization within the meaning of section 5(b) of the War Powers Resolution." It also requires the President to make periodic reports to Congress "on matters relevant to this joint resolution." Finally, the statute expresses Congress' "support" for the efforts of the President to obtain "prompt and decisive action by the Security Council" to enforce Iraq's compliance with all relevant Security Council resolutions.

Public Law 107-243 clearly confers broad authority on the President to use force. In contrast to P.L. 102-1, the authority granted is not limited to the implementation of previously adopted Security Council resolutions concerning Iraq but includes "all relevant ... resolutions." Thus, it appears to incorporate resolutions concerning Iraq that may be adopted by the Security Council in the future as well as those already adopted. The authority also appears to extend beyond compelling Iraq's disarmament to implementing the full range of concerns expressed in those resolutions. Unlike P.L. 107-40, the President's exercise of the authority granted is not dependent upon a finding that Iraq was associated in some direct way with the September 11, 2001, attacks on the U.S. Moreover, the authority conferred can be used for the broad purpose of defending "the national security of the United States against the continuing threat posed by Iraq." Nevertheless, P.L. 107-243 is narrower than P.L. 107-40 in that it limits the authorization for the use of force to Iraq. It also requires as a predicate for the use of force that the President determine that peaceful means cannot suffice and that the use of force against Iraq is consistent with the battle against terrorism. It further limits the force used to that which the President determines is "necessary and appropriate." Finally, as with P.L. 107-40, the statutory authorization for use of force granted to the President in P.L. 107-243 is not dependent for its exercise upon prior authorization by the U.N. Security Council. In the form that P.L. 107-243 is drafted, and given the context in which it was debated, one could argue that it is a classic example of an authorization vehicle contemplated by the original War Powers Resolution.

PROPOSED AMENDMENTS

After 34 years of experience with it in practice, controversy continues over the War Powers Resolution's effectiveness and appropriateness as a system for maintaining a congressional role in the use of armed forces in conflict. One view is that the War Powers Resolution is basically sound and does not need amendment.[86] Those who hold this opinion believe it has brought about better communication between the two branches in times of crisis, and has given Congress a vehicle by which it can act when a majority of Members wish to do so. The Resolution served as a restraint on the use of armed forces by the President in some cases because of awareness that certain actions might invoke its provisions. For example, the threat of invoking the War Powers Resolution may have been helpful in getting U.S. forces out of Grenada, in keeping the number of military advisers in El Salvador limited to 55, and in prodding Congress to take a stand on authorizing the war against Iraq.

A contrary view is that the War Powers Resolution is an inappropriate instrument that restricts the President's effectiveness in foreign policy and should be repealed.[87] Those with this perspective believe that the basic premise of the War Powers Resolution is wrong because in it,Congress attempts excessive control of the deployment of U.S. military forces, encroaching on the responsibility of the President.[88] Supporters of repeal contend that the President needs more flexibility in the conduct of foreign policy and that the time limitation in the War Powers Resolution is unconstitutional and impractical. Some holding this view contend that

Congress has always had the power, through appropriations and general lawmaking, to inquire into, support, limit, or prohibit specific uses of U.S. Armed Forces if there is majority support. The War Powers Resolution does not fundamentally change this equation, it is argued, but it complicates action, misleads military opponents, and diverts attention from key policy questions.

A third view is that the War Powers Resolution has not been adequate to accomplish its objectives and needs to be strengthened or reshaped.[89] Proponents of this view assert that Presidents have continued to introduce U.S. armed forces into hostilities without consulting Congress and without congressional authorization. Presidents have cited section 4(a)(1) on only one occasion — Mayaguez — and by the time the action was reported, it was virtually over.

Holders of this third view have proposed various types of amendments to the War Powers Resolution. These include returning to the version originally passed by the Senate, establishing a congressional consultation group, adding a cutoff of funds, and providing for judicial review. A general discussion of these categories of possible changes follows.

Return to Senate Version: Enumerating Exceptions for Emergency Use

In 1977, Senator Thomas Eagleton proposed that the War Powers Resolution return to the original language of the version passed by the Senate, and this proposal has been made several times since. This would require prior congressional authorization for the introduction of forces into conflict abroad without a declaration of war except to respond to or forestall an armed attack against the United States or its forces or to protect U.S. citizens while evacuating them. The amendment would eliminate the construction that the President has 60 to 90 days in which he can militarily act without authorization. Opponents fear the exceptions to forestall attacks or rescue American citizens abroad would serve as a blanket authorization and might be abused, yet might not allow the needed speed of action and provide adequate flexibility in other circumstances.

Shorten or Eliminate Time Limitation

Another proposal is to shorten the time period that the President could maintain forces in hostile situations abroad without congressional authorization from 60 to 30 days, or eliminate it altogether. Some proponents of this amendment contend the current War Powers Resolution gives the President 60 to 90 days to do as he chooses and that this provides too much opportunity for mischief or irreversible action. The original Senate version provided that the use of armed forces in hostilities or imminent hostilities in any of the emergency situations could not be sustained beyond 30 days without specific congressional authorization, extendable by the President upon certification of necessity for safe disengagement. Opponents of this and related measures argue that they induce military opponents to adopt strategies to win given conflicts in Congress that they could not win in the field over time.

Replace Automatic Withdrawal Requirement

The War Powers Resolution has an automatic requirement for withdrawal of troops 60 days after the President submits a section 4(a)(1) report. Some Members of Congress favor replacing this provision with expedited procedures for a joint resolution to authorize the action or require disengagement. One of the main executive branch objections to the War Powers Resolution has been that the withdrawal requirement could be triggered by congressional inaction, and that adversaries can simply wait out the 60 days. By providing for withdrawal by joint resolution, this amendment would also deal with the provision for withdrawal by concurrent resolution, under a cloud because of the *Chadha* decision. On the other hand, a joint resolution requiring disengagement could be vetoed by the President and thus would require a two-thirds majority vote in both Houses for enactment.

Cutoff of Funds

Some proposals call for prohibiting the obligation or expenditure of funds for any use of U.S. armed forces in violation of the War Powers Resolution or laws passed under it except for the purpose of removing troops.[90] Congress could enforce this provision by refusing to appropriate further funds to continue the militaryaction. This has always been the case, some contend, and would not work because Congress would remain reluctant to withhold financial support for U.S. Armed Forces once they were abroad.

Elimination of Action by Concurrent Resolution

Many proposed amendments eliminate section 5(c) providing that U.S. forces engaged in hostilities abroad without congressional authorization are to be removed if Congress so directs by concurrent resolution, and section 7 providing priority procedures for a concurrent resolution. Those who hold this view contend the concurrent resolution section is invalid because of the *Chadha* decision.

Expedited Procedures

Several proposals call for new and more detailed priority procedures for joint resolutions introduced under the War Powers Resolution. These would apply to joint resolutions eitherauthorizingamilitary action or calling for the withdrawal of forces, and to congressional action to sustain or override a Presidential veto of the joint resolution.[91]

Consultation Group

Several proposed amendments have focused on improving consultation under the War Powers Resolution, particularly by establishing a specific consultation group in Congress for this purpose. Senators Byrd, Nunn, Warner, and Mitchell have proposed the President regularly consult with an initial group of 6 Members — the majority and minority leaders of both Chambers plus the Speaker of the House and President pro tempore of the Senate. Upon a request from a majority of this core group, the President is to consult with a permanent consultative group of 18 Members consisting of the leadership and the ranking and minority members of the Committees on Foreign Relations, Armed Services, and Intelligence. The permanent consultative group would also be able to determine that the President should have reported an introduction of forces and to introduce a joint resolution of authorization or withdrawal that would receive expedited procedures.[92]

Other Members have favored a consultation group, but consider that amendment of the War Powers Resolution is not required for Congress to designate such a group.[93] On October 28, 1993, House Foreign Affairs Chairman Lee Hamilton introduced H.R. 3405 to establish a Standing Consultative Group. Its purpose would be to facilitate improved interaction between the executive branch and Congress on the use of U.S. military forces abroad, including under the War Powers Resolution or United Nations auspices. Members of the Consultative Group would be appointed by the Speaker of the House and the MajorityLeader of the Senate, after consultation with the minority leaders. The Group would include majority and minority representatives of the leadership and the committees on foreign policy, armed services, intelligence, and appropriations.

Another proposal would attempt to improve consultation by broadening the instances in which the President is required to consult. This proposal would cover all situations in which a President is required to report, rather than only circumstances that invoke the time limitation, as is now the case.[94]

Judicial Review

Proposals have been made that any Member of Congress may bring an action in the United States District Court for the District of Columbia for judgment and injunctive relief on the grounds that the President or the U.S. Armed Forces have not complied with any provision of the War Powers Resolution. The intent of this legislation is to give standing to Members to assert the interest of the House or Senate, but whether it would impel courts to exercise jurisdiction is uncertain. Most recent Federal court decisions have rejected War Powers lawsuits by Congressional litigants on the grounds they lacked standing to sue. Proposals have also called for the court not to decline to make a determination on the merits, on the grounds that the issue of compliance is a political question or otherwise nonjusticiable; to accord expedited consideration to the matter; and to prescribe judicial remedies including that the President submit a report or remove Armed Forces from a situation.[95]

Change of Name

Other proposals would construct a Hostilities Act or Use of Force Act and repeal the War Powers Resolution.[96] A possible objection to invoking the War Powers Resolution is reluctance to escalate international tension by implying that a situation is war. Some would see this as a step in the wrong direction; in the Korean and Vietnam conflicts, some contend, it was self-deceptive and ultimately impractical not to recognize hostilities of that magnitude as war and bring to bear the Constitutional provision giving Congress the power to declare war.

United Nations Actions

With the increase in United Nations actions since the end of the Cold War, the question has been raised whether the War Powers Resolution should be amended to facilitate or restrain the President from supplying forces for U.N. actions without congressional approval. Alternatively, the United Nations Participation Act might be amended, or new legislation enacted, to specify how the War Powers Resolution is to be applied, and whether the approval of Congress would be required only for an initial framework agreement on providing forces to the United Nations, or whether Congress would be required to approve an agreement to supply forces in specified situations, particularly for U.N. peacekeeping operations.

APPENDIX A. INSTANCES REPORTED UNDER THE WAR POWERS RESOLUTION

This appendix lists reports Presidents have made to Congress as the result of the War Powers Resolution. Each entry contains the President's reference to the War Powers Resolution.[97] The reports generally cite the President's authority to conduct foreign relations and as Commander in Chief; each entry indicates any additional legislative authority a President cites for his action. Several of the reports listed for the period since 1991, in particular, are reports regarding ongoing operations previously reported by the President, rather than completely new instances of use of the U.S. military overseas.

War Powers Resolution: Presidential Compliance   91

1. **Danang, Vietnam.** On April 4, 1975, President Ford reported the use of naval vessels, helicopters, and Marines to transport refugees from Danang and other seaports to safer areas in Vietnam. His report mentioned section 4(a)(2) of the War Powers Resolution and authorization in the Foreign Assistance Act of 1961 for humanitarian assistance to refugees suffering from the hostilities in South Vietnam. Monroe Leigh, Legal Adviser to the Department of State, testified later that the President "advised the members of the Senate and House leadership that a severe emergency existed in the coastal communities of South Vietnam and that he was directing American naval transports and contract vessels to assist in the evacuation of refugees from coastal seaports."[98]

2. **Cambodia.** On April 12, 1975, President Ford reported the use of ground combat Marines, helicopters, and supporting tactical air elements to assist with the evacuation of U.S. nationals from Cambodia. The report took note of both section 4 and section 4(a)(2) of the War Powers Resolution. On April 3, 1975, the day the President authorized the Ambassador to evacuate the American staff, he directed that the leaders of the Senate and House be advised of the general plan of evacuation. On April 11, the day he ordered the final evacuation, President Ford again directed that congressional leaders be notified.

3. **Vietnam.** On April 30, 1975, President Ford reported the use of helicopters, Marines, and fighter aircraft to aid in the evacuation of U.S. citizens and others from South Vietnam. The report took note of section 4 of the War Powers Resolution. On April 10, the President had asked Congress to clarify its limitation on the use of forces in Vietnam to insure evacuation of U.S. citizens and to cover some Vietnamese nationals, but legislation to this effect was not completed. On April 28, the President directed that congressional leaders be notified that the final phase of the evacuation of Saigon would be carried out by military forces within the next few hours.[99]

4. **Mayaguez.** On May 15, 1975, President Ford reported that he had ordered U.S. military forces to rescue the crew of and retake the ship Mayaguez that had been seized by Cambodian naval patrol boats on May 12, that the ship had been retaken, and that the withdrawal of the

forces had been undertaken. The report took note of section 4(a)(1) of the War Powers Resolution. On May 13, Administration aides contacted 10 Members from the House and 11 Senators regarding the military measures directed by the President.[100]

5. **Iran.** On April 26, 1980, President Carter reported the use of six aircraft and eight helicopters in an unsuccessful attempt of April 24 to rescue the American hostages in Iran. The report was submitted "consistent with the reporting provision" of the War Powers Resolution. President Carter said the United States was acting in accordance with its right under Article 51 of the United Nations Charter to protect and rescueits citizens wherethegovernment of the territory in which they arelocated is unable or unwilling to protect them. The Administration did not inform congressional leaders of the plan on grounds that consultation could endanger the success of the mission.

6. **Sinai.** The United States, Egypt, and Israel signed an executive agreement on August 3, 1981, outlining U.S. participation in a Multinational Force and Observers unit to function as a peacekeeping force in the Sinai after Israel withdrew its forces. In anticipation of this accord, on July 21, 1981, President Reagan requested congressional authorization for U.S. participation. Congress authorized President Reagan to deploy military personnel to the Sinai in the Multinational Force and Observers Participation Resolution, P.L. 97-132, signed December 29, 1981. On March 19, 1982, President Reagan reported the deployment of militarypersonnel and equipment to the Multinational Force and Observers in the Sinai. The President said the report was provided "consistent with section 4(a)(2) of the War Powers Resolution" and cited the Multinational Force and Observers Participation Resolution.

7. **Lebanon.** On August 24, 1982, President Reagan reported the dispatch of 800 Marines to serve in the multinational force to assist in the withdrawal of members of the Palestine Liberation force from Lebanon. The report was provided "consistent with" but did not cite any specific provision of the War Powers Resolution. President Reagan had begun discussions with congressional leaders on July 6,

1982 after the plan had been publicly announced, and after leaks in the Israeli press indicated that he had approved the plan on July 2.[101]

8. **Lebanon.** On September 29, 1982, President Reagan reported the deployment of 1,200 Marines to serve in a temporary multinational force to facilitate the restoration of Lebanese government sovereignty. He said the report was being submitted "consistent with the War Powers Resolution." On this second Multinational Force in Lebanon there was a considerable amount of negotiation between the executive branch and Congress, but most of itoccurred after the decision to participate had been made and the Marines were in Lebanon.[102]

9. **Chad.** On August 8, 1983, President Reagan reported the deployment of two AWACS electronic surveillance planes and eight F-15 fighter planes and ground logistical support forces to Sudan to assist Chad and other friendly governments helping Chad against Libyan and rebel forces. He said the report was being submitted consistent with Section 4 of the War Powers Resolution. On August 23, 1983, a State Department spokesman announced that the planes were being withdrawn.

10. **Lebanon.** On August 30, 1983, after the Marines participating in the Multinational Force in Lebanon were fired upon and two were killed, President Reagan submitted a report "consistent with section 4 of the War Powers Resolution." In P.L.98-119, the Multinational Force in Lebanon Resolution, signed October 12, 1983, Congress determined section 4(a) had become operative on August 29, 1983, and authorized the forces to remain for 18 months.

11. **Grenada.** On October 25, 1983, President Reagan reported that U.S. Army and Marine personnel had begun landing in Grenada to join collective security forces of the Organization of Eastern Caribbean States in assisting in the restoration of law and order in Grenada and to facilitate the protection and evacuation of U.S. citizens. He submitted the report "consistent with the War Powers Resolution." President Reagan met with several congressional leaders at 8 p.m. on October 24.[103] This was after the directive ordering the landing had been signed at 6 p.m., but before the actual invasion that began at 5:30 a.m., October 25.

12. **Libya.** On March 26, 1986, President Reagan reported (without any mention of the War Powers Resolution) that, on March 24 and 25, U.S. forces conducting freedom of navigation exercises in the Gulf of Sidra had been attacked by Libyan missiles. In response, the United States fired missiles at Libyan vessels and at Sirte, the missile site.

13. **Libya.** On April 16, 1986, President Reagan reported, "consistent with the War Powers Resolution", that on April 14 U.S. air and naval forces had conducted bombing strikes on terrorist facilities and military installations in Libya. President Reagan had invited approximately a dozen congressional leaders to the White House at about 4 p.m. on April 14 and discussed the situation until 6 p.m. He indicated that he had ordered the bombing raid and that the aircraft from the United Kingdom were on their way to Libya and would reach their targets about 7 p.m.

14. **Persian Gulf** [104]. On September 23, 1987, President Reagan reported that, on September 21, two U.S. helicopters had fired on an Iranian landing craft observed laying mines in the Gulf. The President said that while mindful of legislative-executive differences on the interpretation and constitutionality of certain provisions of the War Powers Resolution, he was reporting in a spirit of mutual cooperation.

15. **Persian Gulf.** On October 10, 1987, President Reagan reported "consistent with the War Powers Resolution" that, on October 8, three U.S. helicopters were fired upon by small Iranian naval vessels and the helicopters returned fire and sank one of the vessels.

16. **Persian Gulf.** On October 20, 1987, President Reagan reported an attack by an Iranian Silkworm missile against the U.S.-flag tanker Sea Isle City on October 15 and U.S. destruction, on October 19, of the Iranian Rashadat armed platform used to support attacks and mine-laying operations. The report was submitted "consistent with the War Powers Resolution."

17. **Persian Gulf.** On April 19, 1988, President Reagan reported "consistent with the War Powers Resolution" that in response to the U.S.S. Samuel B. Roberts striking a mine on April 14, U.S. Armed Forces attacked and "neutralized" two Iranian oil platforms on April

18 and, after further Iranian attacks, damaged or sank Iranian vessels. The President called the actions "necessary and proportionate." Prior to this action, the President met with congressional leaders.

18. **Persian Gulf.** On July 4, 1988, President Reagan reported that on July 3 the USS Vincennes and USS Elmer Montgomery fired upon approaching Iranian small craft, sinking two. Firing in self-defense at what it believed to be a hostile Iranian military aircraft, the Vincennes had shot down an Iranian civilian airliner. The President expressed deep regret. The report was submitted "consistent with the War Powers Resolution."

19. **Persian Gulf.** On July 14, 1988, President Reagan reported that, on July 12, two U.S. helicopters, responding to a distress call from a Japanese-owned Panamanian tanker, were fired at by two small Iranian boats and returned the fire. The report was submitted "consistent with the War Powers Resolution."

20. **Philippines.** On December 2, 1989, President George H. W. Bush submitted a report to congressional leaders "consistent with" the War Powers Resolution, describing assistance of combat air patrols to help the Aquino government in the Philippines restore order and to protect American lives. After the planes had taken off from Clark Air Base to provide air cover, Vice President Quayle and other officials informed congressional leaders. On December 7, House Foreign Affairs Committee Chairman Dante Fascell wrote President Bush expressing his concern for the lack of advance consultation. In reply, on February 10, 1990, National Security Adviser Brent Scowcroft wrote Chairman Fascell that the President was "committed to consultations with Congress prior to deployments of U.S. Forces into actual or imminent hostilities in all instances where such consultations are possible. In this instance, the nature of the rapidly evolving situation required an extremely rapid decision very late at night and consultation was simply not an option."

21. **Panama.** On December 21, 1989, President George H. W. Bush reported "consistent with theWar Powers Resolution" that he had ordered U.S. military forces to Panama to protect the lives of American citizens and bring General Noriega to justice. By February

13, 1990, all the invasion forces had been withdrawn. President Bush informed several congressional leaders of the approaching invasion of Panama at 6 p.m. on December 19, 1989. This was after the decision to take action was made, but before the operation actually began at 1:00 a.m., December 20.

22. **Liberia.** On August 6, 1990, President George H. W. Bush reported to Congress that following discussions with congressional leaders, a reinforced rifle company had been sent to provide additional security to the U.S. Embassy in Monrovia and helicopter teams had evacuated U.S. citizens from Liberia. The report did not mention the War Powers Resolution or cite any authority.

23. **Iraq.** On August 9, 1990, President George H. W. Bush reported to Congress "consistent with the War Powers Resolution" that he had ordered the forward deployment of substantial elements of the U.S. Armed Forces into the Persian Gulf region to help defend Saudi Arabia after the invasion of Kuwait by Iraq. The Bush Administration notified congressional leaders that it was deploying U.S. troops to Saudi Arabia on August 7, the date of the deployment. After the forces had been deployed, President Bush held several meetings with congressional leaders and members of relevant committees, and committees held hearings to discuss the situation.

24. **Iraq.** On November 16, 1990, President George H. W. Bush reported, without mention of the War Powers Resolution but referring to the August 9 letter, the continued buildup to ensure "an adequate offensive military option." Just prior to adjournment, Senate Majority Leader Mitchell and Speaker Foley designated Members to form a consultation group, and the President held meetings with the group on some occasions, but he did not consult the members in advance on the major buildup of forces in the Persian Gulf area announced November 8.

25. **Iraq.** On January 18, 1991, President George H. W. Bush reported to Congress "consistent with the War Powers Resolution" that he had directed U.S. Armed Forces to commence combat operations on January 16 against Iraqi forces and military targets in Iraq and Kuwait. On January 12, Congress had passed the Authorization for

War Powers Resolution: Presidential Compliance 97

Use of Military Force against Iraq Resolution (P.L. 102-1), which stated it was the specific statutory authorization required by the War Powers Resolution. P.L. 102-1 required the President to submit a report to the Congress at least once every 60 days on the status of efforts to obtain compliance by Iraq with the U.N. Security Council resolution, and Presidents submitted subsequent reports on military actions in Iraq "consistent with" P.L. 102-1. An exception is report submitted June 28, 1993, described below.

26. **Somalia.** On December 10, 1992, President George H. W. Bush reported "consistent with the War Powers Resolution" that U.S. armed forces had entered Somalia on December 8 in response to a humanitarian crisis and a U.N. Security Council Resolution determining that the situation constituted a threat to international peace. He included as authority applicable treaties and laws, and said he had also taken into account views expressed in H.Con.Res. 370, S.Con.Res. 132, and the Horn of Africa Recovery and Food Security Act, P.L. 102-274. On December 4, the day the President ordered the forces deployed, he briefed a number of congressional leaders on the action.

27. **Bosnia.** On April 13, 1993, President Clinton reported "consistent with Section 4 of the War Powers Resolution" that U.S. forces were participating in a NATO air action to enforce a U.N. ban on all unauthorized military flights over Bosnia-Hercegovina, pursuant to his authority as Commander in Chief. Later, on April 27, President Clinton consulted with about two dozen congressional leaders on potential further action.

28. **Somalia.** On June 10, 1993, President Clinton reported that in response to attacks against U.N. forces in Somalia by a factional leader, the U.S. Quick Reaction Force in the area had participated in military action to quell the violence. He said the report was "consistent with the War Powers Resolution, in light of the passage of 6 months since President Bush's initial report...." He said the action was in accordance with applicable treaties and laws, and said the deployment was consistent with S.J.Res. 45 as adopted bythe Senate and amended by the House. (The Senate did not act on the House amendment, so Congress did not take final action on S.J.Res. 45.)

29. **Iraq.** On June 28, 1993, President Clinton reported "consistent with the War Powers Resolution" that on June 26 U.S. naval forces had launched missiles against the Iraqi Intelligence Service's headquarters in Baghdad in response to an unsuccessful attempt to assassinate former President Bush in Kuwait in April 1993.

30. **Macedonia**[105]. On July 9, 1993, President Clinton reported "consistent with Section 4 of the War Powers Resolution" the deployment of approximately 350 U.S. armed forces to Macedonia to participate in the U.N. Protection Force to help maintain stability in the area of former Yugoslavia. He said the deployment was directed in accordance with Section 7 of the United Nations Participation Act.

31. **Bosnia.** On October 13, 1993, President Clinton reported "consistent with the War Powers Resolution" that U.S. military forces continued to support enforcement of the U.N. no-fly zone in Bosnia, noting that more that 50 U.S. aircraft were now available for NATO efforts in this regard.

32. **Haiti.** On October 20, 1993, President Clinton submitted a report "consistent with the War Powers Resolution" that U.S. ships had begun to enforce a U.N. embargo against Haiti.

33. **Macedonia.** On January 8, 1994, President Clinton reported "consistent with the War Powers Resolution" that approximately 300 members of a reinforced company team (RCT) of the U.S. Army's 3rd Infantry Division (Mechanized) had assumed a peacekeeping role in Macedonia as part of the United Nations Protection Force (UNPROFOR) on January 6, 1994.

34. **Bosnia.** On February 17, 1994, President Clinton reported "consistent with the War Powers Resolution" that the United States had expanded its participation in United Nations and NATO efforts to reach a peaceful solution in former Yugoslavia and that 60 U.S. aircraft were available for participation in the authorized NATO missions.

35. **Bosnia.** On March 1, 1994, President Clinton reported "consistent with" the War Powers Resolution that on February 28 U.S. planes patrolling the "no-fly zone" in former Yugoslavia under the North

Atlantic Treaty Organization (NATO) shot down 4 Serbian Galeb planes.

36. **Bosnia.** On April 12, 1994, President Clinton reported "consistent with" the War Powers Resolution that on April 10 and 11, U.S. warplanes under NATO command had fired against Bosnian Serb forces shelling the "safe" city of Gorazde.

37. **Rwanda.** On April 12, 1994, President Clinton reported "consistent with" the War Powers Resolution that combat-equipped U.S. military forces had been deployed to Burundi to conduct possible non-combatant evacuation operations of U.S. citizens and other third-country nationals from Rwanda, where widespread fighting had broken out.

38. **Macedonia.** On April 19, 1994, President Clinton reported "consistent with the War Powers Resolution" that the U.S. contingent in the former Yugoslav Republic of Macedonia had been augmented by a reinforced company of 200 personnel.

39. **Haiti.** On April 20, 1994, President Clinton reported "consistent with the War Powers Resolution" that U.S. naval forces had continued enforcement in the waters around Haiti and that 712 vessels had been boarded.

40. **Bosnia.** On August 22, 1994, President Clinton reported the use on August 5 of U.S. aircraft under NATO to attack Bosnian Serb heavy weapons in the Sarajevo heavy weapons exclusion zone upon request of the U.N. Protection Forces. He did not cite the War Powers Resolution but referred to the April 12 report that cited the War Powers Resolution.

41. **Haiti.** On September 21, 1994, President Clinton reported "consistent with the War Powers Resolution" the deployment of 1,500 troops to Haiti to restore democracy in Haiti. The troop level was subsequently increased to 20,000.

42. **Bosnia.** On November 22, 1994, President Clinton reported "consistent with the War Powers Resolution" the use of U.S. combat

aircraft on November 21, 1994 under NATO to attack bases used by Serbs to attack the town of Bihac in Bosnia.

43. **Macedonia.** On December 22, 1994, President Clinton reported "consistent with the War Powers Resolution" that the U.S. Army contingent in the former Yugoslav Republic of Macedonia continued its peacekeeping mission and that the current contingent would soon be replaced by about 500 soldiers from the 3rd Battalion, 5th Cavalry Regiment, 1st Armored Division from Kirchgons, Germany.

44. **Somalia.** On March 1, 1995, President Clinton reported "consistent with the War Powers Resolution" that on February 27, 1995, 1,800 combat-equipped U.S. armed forces personnel began deployment into Mogadishu, Somalia, to assist in the withdrawal of U.N. forces assigned thereto theUnited Nations Operation in Somalia (UNOSOM II).

45. **Haiti.** On March 21, 1995, President Clinton reported "consistent with the War Powers Resolution" that U.S. military forces in Haiti as part of a U.N. Multinational Force had been reduced to just under 5,300 personnel. He noted that as of March 31, 1995, approximately 2,500 U.S. personnel would remain in Haiti as part of the U.N. Mission in Haiti UNMIH).

46. **Bosnia.** On May 24, 1995, President Clinton reported "consistent with the War Powers Resolution" that U.S. combat-equipped fighter aircraft and other aircraft continued to contribute to NATO's enforcement of the no-fly zone in airspace over Bosnia-Herzegovina. U.S. aircraft, he noted, are also available for close air support of U.N. forces in Croatia. Roughly 500 U.S. soldiers continue to be deployed in the former Yugoslav Republic of Macedonia as part of the U.N. Preventive Deployment Force (UNPREDEP). U.S. forces continue to support U.N. refugee and embargo operations in this region.

47. **Bosnia.** On September 1, 1995, President Clinton reported "consistent with the War Powers Resolution," that "U.S. combat and support aircraft" had been used beginning on August 29, 1995, in a series of NATO air strikes against Bosnian Serb Army (BSA) forces in Bosnia-Herzegovina that were threatening the U.N.-declared safe areas of

Sarajevo, Tuzla, and Gorazde." He noted that during the first day of operations, "some 300 sorties were flown against 23 targets in the vicinity of Sarajevo, Tuzla, Goradzde and Mostar."

48. **Haiti.** On September 21, 1995, President Clinton reported "consistent with the War Powers Resolution" that currently the United States has 2,400 military personnel in Haiti as participants in the U.N. Mission in Haiti (UNMIH). In addition, 260 U.S. military personnel are assigned to the U.S. Support Group Haiti.

49. **Bosnia.** On December 6, 1995, President Clinton notified Congress, "consistent with the War Powers Resolution," that he had "ordered the deployment of approximately 1,500 U.S. military personnel to Bosnia and Herzegovina and Croatia as part of a NATO 'enabling force' to lay the groundwork for the prompt and safe deployment of the NATO-led Implementation Force (IFOR)," which would be used to implement the Bosnian peace agreement after its signing. The President also noted that he had authorized deployment of roughly 3,000 other U.S. military personnel to Hungary, Italy, and Croatia to establish infrastructure for the enabling force and the IFOR.

50. **Bosnia.** On December 21, 1995, President Clinton notified Congress "consistent with the War Powers Resolution" that he had ordered the deployment of approximately 20,000 U.S. military personnel to participate in the NATO-led Implementation Force (IFOR) in the Republic of Bosnia-Herzegovina, and approximately 5,000 U.S. military personnel would be deployed in other former Yugoslav states, primarily in Croatia. In addition, about 7,000 U.S. support forces would be deployed to Hungary, Italy and Croatia and other regional states in support of IFOR's mission. The President ordered participation of U.S. forces "pursuant to" his "constitutional authority to conduct the foreign relations of the United States and as Commander-in-Chief and Chief Executive."

51. **Haiti.** On March 21, 1996, President Clinton notified Congress "consistent with the War Powers Resolution" that beginning in January 1996 there had been a "phased reduction" in the number of United States personnel assigned to the United Nations Mission in

Haiti (UNMIH). As of March 21, 309 U.S. personnel remained a part of UNMIH. These U.S. forces were "equipped for combat."

52. **Liberia.** On April 11, 1996, President Clinton notified Congress "consistent with the War Powers Resolution" that on April 9, 1996 due to the "deterioration of the security situation and the resulting threat to American citizens" in Liberia he had ordered U.S. military forces to evacuate from that country "private U.S. citizens and certain third-country nationals who had taken refuge in the U.S. Embassy compound...."

53. **Liberia.** On May 20, 1996, President Clinton notified Congress, "consistent with the War Powers Resolution" of the continued deployment of U.S. military forces in Liberia to evacuate both American citizens and other foreign personnel, and to respond to various isolated "attacks on the American Embassy complex" in Liberia. The President noted that the deployment of U.S. forces would continue until therewas no longer any need for enhanced security at the Embassy and a requirement to maintain an evacuation capability in the country.

54. **Central African Republic.** On May 23, 1996, President Clinton notified Congress, "consistent with the War Powers Resolution" of the deployment of U.S. military personnel to Bangui, Central African Republic, to conduct the evacuation from that country of "private U.S. citizens and certain U.S. Government employees," and to provide "enhanced security" for the American Embassy in Bangui.

55. **Bosnia.** On June 21, 1996, President Clinton notified Congress, "consistent with the War Powers Resolution" that United States forces totalingabout 17,000 remain deployed in Bosnia "under NATO operational command and control" as part of the NATO Implementation Force (IFOR). In addition, about 5,500 U.S. military personnel are deployed in Hungary, Italy and Croatia, and other regional states to provide "logistical and other support to IFOR." The President noted that it was the intention that IFOR would complete the withdrawal of all troops in the weeks after December 20, 1996, on a schedule "set by NATO commanders consistent with the safety of troops and the logistical requirements for an orderly withdrawal." He

also noted that a U.S. Army contingent (of about 500 U.S. soldiers) remains in the Former Yugoslav Republic of Macedonia as part of the United Nations Preventive Deployment Force (UNPREDEP).

56. **Rwanda and Zaire.** On December 2, 1996, President Clinton notified Congress "consistent with the War Powers Resolution," that in support of the humanitarian efforts of the United Nations regarding refugees in Rwanda and the Great Lakes Region of Eastern Zaire, he had authorized the use of U.S. personnel and aircraft, including AC-130U planes to help in surveying the region in support of humanitarian operations, although fighting still was occurring in the area, and U.S. aircraft had been subject to fire when on flight duty.

57. **Bosnia.** On December 20, 1996, President Clinton notified Congress "consistent with the War Powers Resolution," that he had authorized U.S. participation in an IFOR follow-on force in Bosnia, known as SFOR (Stabilization Force), under NATO command. The President said the U.S. forces contribution to SFOR was to be "about 8,500" personnel whose primary mission was to deter or prevent a resumption of hostilities or new threats to peace in Bosnia. SFOR's duration was Bosnia is expected to be 18 months, with progressive reductions and eventual withdrawal.

58. **Albania.** On March 15, 1997, President Clinton notified Congress "consistent with the War Powers Resolution," that on March 13, 1997, he had utilized U.S. military forces to evacuate certain U.S. Government employees and private U.S. citizens from Tirana, Albania, and to enhance security for the U.S. embassy in that city.

59. **Congo and Gabon.** On March 27, 1997, President Clinton notified Congress "consistent with the War Powers Resolution," that on March 25, 1997, a standbyevacuation force of U.S. military personnel had been deployed to Congo and Gabon to provide enhanced security for American private citizens, government employees and selected third country nationals in Zaire, and be available for any necessary evacuation operation.

60. **Sierra Leone.** On May 30, 1997, President Clinton notified Congress "consistent with the War Powers Resolution," that on May 29 and

May 30, 1997, U.S. military personnel were deployed to Freetown, Sierra Leone to prepare for and undertake the evacuation of certain U.S. Government employees and private U.S. citizens.

61. **Bosnia.** On June 20, 1997, President Clinton notified Congress "consistent with the War Powers Resolution," that U.S. Armed Forces continued to support peacekeeping operations in Bosnia and other states in the region in support of the NATO-led Stabilization Force (SFOR). He reported that most U.S. military personnel then involved in SFOR were in Bosnia, near Tuzla, and about 2,800 U.S. troops were deployed in Hungary, Croatia, Italy, and other regional states to provide logistics and other support to SFOR. A U.S. Army contingent of about 500 also remained deployed in the Former Yugoslav Republic of Macedonia as part of the U.N. Preventative Deployment Force (UNPREDEP).

62. **Cambodia.** On July 11, 1997, President Clinton notified Congress "consistent with the War Powers Resolution," that in an effort to ensure the security of American citizens in Cambodia during a period of domestic conflict there, he had deployed a Task Force of about 550 U.S. military personnel to Utapao Air Base in Thailand. These personnel were to be available for possible emergency evacuation operations in Cambodia.

63. **Bosnia.** On December 19, 1997, President Clinton notified Congress "consistent with the War Powers Resolution," that he intended "in principle" to have the United States participate in a security presence in Bosnia when the NATO SFOR contingent withdrew in the summer of 1998.

64. **Guinea-Bissau.** On June 12, 1998 President Clinton reported to Congress "consistent with the War Powers Resolution" that, on June 10, 1998, in response to an army mutiny in Guinea-Bissau endangering the U.S. Embassy and U.S. government employees and citizens in that country, he had deployed a standby evacuation force of U.S. military personnel to Dakar, Senegal, to remove such individuals, as well as selected third country nationals, from the city of Bissau.

65. **Bosnia.** On June 19, 1998, President Clinton reported to Congress "consistent with the War Powers Resolution" regarding activities in the last six months of combat-equipped U.S. forces in support of NATO's SFOR in Bosnia and surrounding areas of former Yugoslavia.

66. **Kenya and Tanzania.** On August 10, 1998, President Clinton reported to Congress "consistent with the War Powers Resolution" that he had deployed, on August 7, 1998, a Joint Task Force of U.S. military personnel to Nairobi, Kenya to coordinate the medical and disaster assistance related to the bombings of the U.S. embassies in Kenya and Tanzania. He also reported that teams of 50-100 security personnel had arrived in Nairobi, Kenya and Dar es Salaam, Tanzania to enhance the security of the U.S. embassies and citizens there.

67. **Albania.** On August 18, 1998, President Clinton reported to Congress, "consistent with the War Powers Resolution," that he had, on August 16, 1998, deployed 200 U.S. Marines and 10 Navy SEALS to the U.S. Embassy compound in Tirana, Albania to enhance security against reported threats against U.S. personnel.

68. **Afghanistan and Sudan.** On August 21, 1998, by letter, President Clinton notified Congress "consistent with the War Powers Resolution" that he had authorized airstrikes on August 20th against camps and installations in Afghanistan and Sudan used by the Osama bin Laden terrorist organization. The President did so based on what he termed convincing information that the bin Laden organization was responsible for the bombings, on August 7, 1998, of the U.S. embassies in Kenya and Tanzania.

69. **Liberia.** On September 29, 1998, by letter, President Clinton notified Congress "consistent with the War Powers Resolution" that he had deployed a stand-by response and evacuation force to Liberia to augment the security force at the U.S. Embassy in Monrovia, and to provide for a rapid evacuation capability, as needed, to remove U.S. citizens and government personnel from the country.

70. **Bosnia.** On January 19, 1999, by letter, President Clinton notified Congress "consistent with theWar Powers Resolution" that pursuant to his authority as Commander-in-Chief he was continuing to

authorize the use of combat-equipped U.S. Armed Forces to Bosnia and other states in the region to participate in and support the NATO-led Stabilization Force (SFOR). He noted that U.S. SFOR military personnel totaled about 6,900, with about 2,300 U.S. military personnel deployed to Hungary, Croatia, Italy and other regional states. Also some 350 U.S. military personnel remain deployed in the Former Yugoslav Republic of Macedonia (FYROM) as part of the UN Preventative Deployment Force (UNPREDEP).

71. **Kenya.** On February 25, 1999, President Clinton submitted a supplemental report to Congress "consistent with the War Powers Resolution" describing the continuing deployment of U.S. military personnel in Kenya to provide continuing security for U.S. embassy and American citizens in Nairobi in the aftermath of the terrorist bombing there.

72. **Yugoslavia/Kosovo.** On March 26, 1999, President Clinton notified Congress "consistent with the War Powers Resolution," that on March 24, 1999, U.S. militaryforces, at his direction and acting jointly with NATO allies, had commenced air strikes against Yugoslavia in response to the Yugoslav government's campaign of violence and repression against the ethnic Albanian population in Kosovo.

73. **Yugoslavia/Albania.** On April 7, 1999, President Clinton notified Congress, "consistent with the War Powers Resolution," that he had ordered additional U.S. military forces to Albania, including rotary wing aircraft, artillery, and tactical missiles systems to enhance NATO's ability to conduct effective air operations in Yugoslavia. About 2,500 soldiers and aviators are to be deployed as part of this task force.

74. **Yugoslavia/Albania.** On May 25, 1999, President Clinton reported to Congress, "consistent with the War Powers Resolution" that he had directed "deployment of additional aircraft and forces to support NATO's ongoing efforts [against Yugoslavia], including several thousand additional U.S. Armed Forces personnel to Albania in support of the deep strike force located there." He also directed that additional U.S. forces be deployed to the region to assist in "humanitarian operations."

75. **Yugoslavia/Kosovo.** On June 12, 1999, President Clinton reported to Congress, "consistent with the War Powers Resolution," that he had directed the deployment of about "7,000 U.S. military personnel as the U.S. contribution to the approximately 50,000-member, NATO-led security force (KFOR)" currently being assembled in Kosovo. He also noted that about "1,500 U.S. military personnel, under separate U.S. command and control, will deploy to other countries in the region, as our national support element, in support of KFOR."

76. **Bosnia.** On July 19, 1999, President Clinton reported to Congress "consistent with the War Powers Resolution" that about 6,200 U.S. military personnel were continuing to participate in the NATO-led Stabilization Force (SFOR) in Bosnia, and that another 2,200 personnel were supporting SFOR operations from Hungary, Croatia, and Italy. He also noted that U.S. military personnel remain in the Former Yugoslav Republic of Macedonia to support the international security presence in Kososo (KFOR).

77. **East Timor.** On October 8, 1999, President Clinton reported to Congress "consistent with the War Powers Resolution" that he had directed the deployment of a limited number of U.S. military forces to East Timor to support the U.N. multinational force (INTERFET) aimed at restoring peace to East Timor. U.S. support had been limited initiallyto "communications, logistics, planning assistance and transportation." The President further noted that he had authorized deployment of the amphibious ship USS BELLEAU WOOD, together with its helicopters and her complement of personnel from the 31st Marine Expeditionary Unit (Special Operations Capable) (MEU SOC)) to the East Timor region, to provide helicopter airlift and search and rescue support to the multinational operation. U.S. participation was anticipated to continue until the transition to a U.N. peacekeeping operation was complete.

78. **Yugoslavia/Kosovo.** On December 15, 1999, President Clinton reported to Congress "consistent with the War Powers Resolution" that U.S. combat-equipped military personnel continued to serve as part of the NATO-led security force in Kosovo (KFOR). He noted that the American contribution to KFOR in Kosovo was "approximately8,500 U.S. militarypersonnel." U.S. forces were

deployed in a sector centered around "Urosevac in the eastern portion of Kosovo." For U.S. KFOR forces, "maintaining public security is a key task." Other U.S. military personnel are deployed to other countries in the region to serve in administrative and logistics support roles for U.S. forces in KFOR. Of these forces, about 1,500 U.S. military personnel are in Macedonia and Greece, and occasionally in Albania.

79. **Bosnia.** On January 25, 2000, President Clinton reported to Congress "consistent with the War Powers Resolution" that the U.S. continued to provide combat-equipped U.S. Armed Forces to Bosnia and Herzegovina and other states in the region as part of the NATO led Stabilization Force (SFOR). The President noted that the U.S. force contribution was being reduced from "approximately 6,200 to 4,600 personnel," with the U.S. forces assigned to Multinational Division, North, centered around the city of Tuzla. He added that approximately 1,500 U.S. military personnel were deployed to Hungary, Croatia, and Italy to provide "logistical and other support to SFOR," and that U.S. forces continue to support SFOR in "efforts to apprehend persons indicted for war crimes."

80. **East Timor.** On February 25, 2000, President Clinton reported to Congress "consistent with the War Powers Resolution" that he had authorized the participation of a small number of U.S. military personnel in support of the United Nations Transitional Administration in East Timor (UNTAET), with a mandate to maintain law and order throughout East Timor, facilitate establishment of an effective administration there, deliver humanitarian assistance, and support the building of self-government. The President reported that the U.S. contingent was small: three military observers, and one judge advocate. To facilitate and coordinate U.S. military activities in East Timor, the President also authorized the deployment of a support group (USGET), consisting of 30 U.S. personnel. U.S. personnel would be temporarily deployed to East Timor, on a rotational basis, and through periodic ship visits, during which U.S. forces would conduct "humanitarian and assistance activities throughout East Timor." Rotational activities should continue through the summer of 2000.

War Powers Resolution: Presidential Compliance   109

81. **Sierra Leone.** On May 12, 2000, President Clinton, "consistent with the War Powers Resolution" reported to Congress that he had ordered a U.S. Navypatrol craft to deploy to Sierra Leone to be ready to support evacuation operations from that country if needed. He also authorized a U.S. C-17 aircraft to deliver "ammunition, and other supplies and equipment" to Sierra Leone in support of United Nations peacekeeping operations there.

82. **Yugoslavia/Kosovo.** On June 16, 2000, President Clinton reported to Congress, "consistent with the War Powers Resolution," that the U.S. was continuing to provide military personnel to the NATO-led KFOR security force in Kosovo. U.S. forces were numbered at 7,500, but were scheduled to be reduced to 6,000 when ongoing troop rotations were completed. U.S. forces in Kosovo are assigned to a sector centered near Gnjilane in eastern Kosovo. Other U.S. military personnel are deployed to other countries to serve in administrative and logistics support roles, with approximately 1,000 U.S. personnel in Macedonia, Albania, and Greece.

83. **Bosnia.** On July 25, 2000, President Clinton reported to Congress, "consistent with the War Powers Resolution," that combat-equipped U.S. military personnel continued to participate in the NATO-led Stabilization Force (SFOR) in Bosnia and Herzegovina, being deployed to Bosnia, and other states in the region in support of peacekeeping efforts in former Yugoslavia. U.S. military personnel levels have been reduced from 6,200 to 4,600. Apart from the forces in Bosnia, approximately 1,000 U.S. personnel continue to be deployed in support roles in Hungary, Croatia, and Italy.

84. **East Timor.** On August 25, 2000, President Clinton reported to Congress,"consistent with the War Powers Resolution," that the United States was currently contributing three military observers to the United Nations Transitional Administration in East Timor (UNTAET) that is charged by the UN with restoring and maintaining peace and security there. He also noted that the U.S. was maintaining a military presence in East Timor separate from UNTAET, comprised of about 30 U.S. personnel who facilitate and coordinate U.S. military activities in East Timor and rotational operations of U.S. forces there. U.S. forces currently conduct humanitarian and civic assistance activities for East Timor's citizens. U.S. rotational presence

operations in East Timor are presently expected, the President said, to continue through December 2000.

85. **Yemen.** On October 14, 2000, President Clinton reported to Congress, "consistent with the War Powers Resolution," that on October 12, 2000, in the wake of an attack on the USS COLE in the port of Aden, Yemen, he had authorized deployment of about 45 military personnel from U.S. Naval Forces Central Command to Aden to provide "medical, security, and disaster response assistance." The President further reported that on October 13, 2000 about 50 U.S. military security personnel arrived in Aden, and that additional "security elements" may be deployed to the area, to enhance the ability of the U.S. to ensure the security of the USS COLE and the personnel responding to the incident. In addition, two U.S. Navy surface combatant vessels are operating in or near Yemeni territorial waters to provide communications and other support, as required.

86. **Yugoslavia/Kosovo.** On December 18, 2000, President Clinton reported to Congress, "consistent with the War Powers Resolution," that the United States was continuing to provide approximately 5,600 U.S. military personnel in support of peacekeeping efforts in Kosovo as part of the NATO-led international security force in Kosovo (KFOR). An additional 500 U.S. military personnel are deployed as the National Support Element in Macedonia, with an occasional presence in Albania and Greece. U.S. forces are assigned to a sector centered around Gnjilane in the eastern portion of Kosovo. The President noted that the mission for these U.S. military forces is maintaining a safe and secure environment through conducting "security patrols in urban areas and in the countryside throughout their sector."

87. **Bosnia.** On January 25, 2001, President George W. Bush reported to Congress, "consistent with the War Powers Resolution,"that about 4,400 combat-equipped U.S. Armed Forces continued to be deployed in Bosnia and Herzegovina, and other regional states as part of the NATO-led Stabilization Force (SFOR).Most were based at Tuzla in Bosnia. About 650 others were based in Hungary, Croatia, and Italy, providing logistical and other support.

88. **East Timor.** On March 2, 2001, President George W. Bush reported to Congress, "consistent with the War Powers Resolution," that the U. S. armed forces were continuing to support the United Nations peacekeeping effort in East Timor aimed at providing security and maintaining law and order in East Timor, coordinating delivery of humanitarian assistance, and helping establish the basis for self-government in East Timor. The U.S. currently has three military observers attached to the United Nations Transitional Administration in East Timor (UNTAET). The United States also has a separate military presence, the U.S. Support Group East Timor (USGET), of approximately 12 U.S. personnel, including a security detachment, which "facilitates and coordinates" U.S. military activities in East Timor.

89. **Yugoslavia/Kosovo.** On May 18, 2001, President George W. Bush reported to Congress, "consistent with the War Powers Resolution," that the United States was continuing to provide approximately 6,000 U.S. military personnel in support of peacekeeping efforts in Kosovo as part of the NATO-led international security force in Kosovo (KFOR). An additional 500 U.S. military personnel are deployed as the National Support Element in Macedonia, with an occasional presence in Greece and Albania. U.S. forces in Kosovo are assigned to a sector centered around Gnjilane in the eastern portion. President Bush noted that the mission for these U.S. military forces is maintaining a safe and secure environment through conducting security patrols in urban areas and in the countryside through their sector.

90. **Bosnia.** On July 24, 2001, President George W. Bush reported to Congress, "consistent with the War Powers Resolution," about 3,800 combat-equipped U.S. Armed Forces continued to be deployed in Bosnia and Herzegovina, and other regional states as part of the NATO-led Stabilization Force (SFOR). Most were based at Tuzla in Bosnia. About 500 others were based in Hungary, Croatia, and Italy, providing logistical and other support.

91. **East Timor.** On August 31, 2001, President George W. Bush reported to Congress, "consistent with the War Powers Resolution," that the U. S. armed forces were continuing to support the United Nations

peacekeeping effort in East Timor aimed at providing security and maintaining law and order in East Timor, coordinating delivery of humanitarian assistance, and helping establish the basis for self-government in East Timor. The U.S. currently has three military observers attached to the United Nations Transitional Administration in East Timor (UNTAET). The United States also has a separate military presence, the U.S. Support Group East Timor (USGET), of approximately 20 U.S. personnel, including a security detachment, which "facilitates and coordinates" U.S. military activities in East Timor, as well as a rotational presence of U.S. forces through temporary deployments to East Timor. The President stated that U.S. forces would continue a presence through December 2001, while options for a U.S. presence in 2002 are being reviewed, with the President's objective being redeployment of USGET personnel, as circumstances permit.

92. **Anti-terrorist operations.** On September 24, 2001, President George W. Bush reported to Congress, "consistent with the War Powers Resolution," and "Senate Joint Resolution 23" that in response to terrorist attacks on the World Trade Center and the Pentagon he had ordered the "deployment of various combat-equipped and combat support forces to a number of foreign nations in the Central and Pacific Command areas of operations." The President noted in efforts to "prevent and deter terrorism" he might find it necessary to order additional forces into these and other areas of the world...." He stated that he could not now predict "the scope and duration of these deployments," nor the "actions necessaryto counter the terrorist threat to the United States."

93. **Afghanistan.** On October 9, 2001, President George W. Bush reported to Congress, "consistent with the War Powers Resolution," and "Senate Joint Resolution 23" that on October 7, 2001, U.S. Armed Forces "began combat action in Afghanistan against Al Qaida terrorists and their Taliban supporters." The President stated that he had directed thismilitaryaction in response to the September 11, 2001 attacks on U.S. "territory, our citizens, and our way of life, and to the continuing threat of terrorist acts against the United States and our friends and allies." This military action was "part of our campaign

against terrorism" and was "designed to disrupt the use of Afghanistan as a terrorist base of operations."

94. **Yugoslavia/Kosovo.** On November 19, 2001, President George W. Bush reported to Congress, "consistent with the War Powers Resolution," that the United States was continuing to provide approximately 5,500 U.S. military personnel in support of peacekeeping efforts in Kosovo as part of the NATO-led international security force in Kosovo (KFOR). An additional 500 U.S. military personnel are deployed as the National Support Element in Macedonia, with an occasional presence in Greece and Albania. U.S. forces in Kosovo are assigned to a sector centered around Gnjilane in the eastern portion. President Bush noted that the mission for these U.S. military forces is maintaining a safe and secure environment through conducting security patrols in urban areas and in the countryside through their sector.

95. **Bosnia.** On January 21, 2002, President George W. Bush reported to Congress, "consistent with the War Powers Resolution," that about 3,100 combat-equipped U.S. Armed Forces continued to be deployed in Bosnia and Herzegovina, and other regional states as part of the NATO-led Stabilization Force (SFOR).Most were based at Tuzla in Bosnia. About 500 others were based in Hungary, Croatia, and Italy, providing logistical and other support.

96. **East Timor.** On February 28, 2002, President George W. Bush reported to Congress, "consistent with the War Powers Resolution," that U. S. armed forces were continuing to support the United Nations peacekeeping effort in East Timor aimed at providing security and maintaining law and order in East Timor, coordinating delivery of humanitarian assistance, and helping establish the basis for self-government in East Timor. The U.S. currently has three military observers attached to the United Nations Transitional Administration in East Timor (UNTAET). The United States also has a separate military presence, the U.S. Support Group East Timor (USGET), comprised of approximately 10 U.S. personnel, including a security detachment, which "facilitates and coordinates" U.S. military activities in East Timor, as well as a rotational presence of U.S. forces through temporary deployments to East Timor. The President stated

that U.S. forces would continue a presence through 2002. The President noted his objective was to gradually reduce the "rotational presence operations," and to redeploy USGET personnel, as circumstances permitted.

97. **Anti-terrorist operations.** On March 20, 2002, President George W. Bush reported to Congress, "consistent with the War Powers Resolution,"on U.S. efforts in the "global war on Terrorism." He noted that the "heart of the al-Qaeda training capability" had been "seriously degraded," and that the remainder of the Taliban and the al-Qaeda fighters were being "actively pursued and engaged by the U.S., coalition and Afghan forces." The United States was also conducting "maritime interception operations...to locate and detain suspected al-Qaeda or Taliban leadership fleeing Afghanistan by sea." At the Philippine Government's invitation, the President had ordered deployed "combat-equipped and combat support forces to train with, advise, and assist" the Philippines' Armed Forces in enhancing their "existing counterterrorist capabilities." The strength of U.S. military forces working with the Philippines was projected to be 600 personnel. The President noted that he was "assessing options" for assisting other nations, including Georgia and Yemen, in enhancing their "counterterrorism capabilities, including training and equipping their armed forces." He stated that U.S. combat-equipped and combat support forces would be necessary for these efforts, if undertaken.

98. **Yugoslavia/Kosovo.** On May 17, 2002, President George W. Bush reported to Congress, "consistent with the War Powers Resolution," that the U.S. military was continuing to support peacekeeping efforts of the NATO-led international security force in Kosovo (KFOR). He noted that the current U.S. contribution was about 5,100 military personnel, with an additional 468 personnel in Macedonia; and an occasional presence in Albania and Greece.

99. **Bosnia.** On July 22, 2002, President George W. Bush reported to Congress, "consistent with the War Powers Resolution," that the U.S. military was continuing to support peacekeeping efforts of the NATO-led Stabilization Force (SFOR) in Bosnia and Herzegovina and other regional states. He noted that the current U.S. contribution was "approximately 2,400 personnel." Most U.S. forces in Bosnia and

Herzegovina are assigned to the Multinational Division, North headquartered in Tuzla. An additional 60 U.S. military personnel are deployed to Hungary and Croatia to provide logistical and other support.

100. **Anti-terrorist operations.** On September 20, 2002, President Bush reported to Congress "consistent with the War Powers Resolution," that U.S. "combat-equipped and combat support forces" have been deployed to the Philippines since January 2002 to train with, assist and advise the Philippines' Armed Forces in enhancing their "counterterrorist capabilities." He added that U.S. forces were conducting maritime interception operations in the Central and European Command areas to combat movement, arming, or financing of "international terrorists." He also noted that U.S. combat personnel had been deployed to Georgia and Yemen to help enhance the "counterterrorist capabilities" of their armed forces.

101. **Cote d'Ivoire.** On September 26, 2002, President Bush reported to Congress "consistent with the War Powers Resolution," that in response to a rebellion in Cote d'Ivoire that he had on September 25, 2002 sent U.S. military personnel into Cote d'Ivoire to assist in the evacuation of American citizens and third country nationals from the city of Bouake; and otherwise assist in other evacuations as necessary.

102. **Yugoslavia/Kosovo.** On November 15, 2002, the President reported to Congress "consistent with the War Powers Resolution" that the U.S. was continuing to deploy combat equipped military personnel as part of the NATO-led international security force in Kosovo (KFOR). Currently the U.S. has approximately 4,350 U.S. military personnel in Kosovo, with an additional 266 military personnel in Macedonia. The U.S. also has an occasional presence in Albania and Greece, associated with the KFOR mission.

103. **Bosnia.** On January 21, 2003, President George W. Bush reported to Congress, "consistent with the War Powers Resolution," that about 1,800 U.S. Armed Forces personnel continued to be deployed in Bosnia and Herzegovina, and other regional states as part of the NATO-led Stabilization Force (SFOR). Most were based at Tuzla in Bosnia. About 80 others were based in Hungary and Croatia, providing logistical and other support.

104. **Anti-terrorist operations.** On March 20, 2003, President Bush reported to Congress, "consistent with the War Powers Resolution," as well as P.L. 107-40, and "pursuant to" his authority as Commander-in-Chief, that he had continued a number of U.S. military operations globally in the war against terrorism. These military operations included ongoing U.S. actions against al-Qaeda fighters in Afghanistan; collaborative anti-terror operations with forces of Pakistan in the Pakistan/Afghanistan border area; "maritime interception operations on the high seas" in areas of responsibility of the Central and European Commands to prevent terrorist movement and other activities; and military support for the armed forces of Georgia and Yemen in counter-terrorism operations.

105. **War against Iraq.** On March 21, 2003, President Bush reported to Congress, "consistent with the War Powers Resolution," as well as P.L. 102-1 and P.L. 107-243, and "pursuant to" his authority as Commander-in-Chief, that he had "directed U.S. Armed Forces, operating with other coalition forces, to commence operations on March 19, 2003, against Iraq." He further stated that it was not possible to know at present the duration of active combat operations or the scope necessary to accomplish the goals of the operation — "to disarm Iraq in pursuit of peace, stability, and security both in the Gulf region and in the United States."

106. **Yugoslavia/Kosovo.** On May 14, 2003, President Bush reported to Congress, "consistent with the War Powers Resolution," that combat-equipped U.S. military personnel continued to be deployed as part of the NATO-led international security force in Kosovo (KFOR). He noted that about 2,250 U.S. military personnel were deployed in Kosovo, and additional military personnel operated, on occasion, from Macedonia, Albania, and Greece in support of KFOR operations.

107. **Liberia.** On June 9, 2003, President Bush reported to Congress, "consistent with the War Powers Resolution," that on June 8 he had sent about 35 combat-equipped U.S. military personnel into Monrovia, Liberia, to augment U.S. Embassy security forces, to aid in the possible evacuation of U.S. citizens if necessary. The President also noted that he had sent about 34 combat-equipped U.S. military personnel to help secure the U.S. embassy in Nouakchott, Mauritania,

and to assist in evacuation of American citizens if required. They were expected to arrive at the U.S. embassy by June 10, 2003. Back-up and support personnel were sent to Dakar, Senegal, to aid in any necessary evacuation from either Liberia or Mauritania.

108. **Bosnia.** On July 22, 2003, President Bush reported to Congress, "consistent with the War Powers Resolution," that the United States continued to provide about 1,800 combat-equipped militarypersonnel in Bosnia and Herzegovina in support of NATO's Stabilization Force (SFOR) and its peacekeeping efforts in this country.

109. **Liberia.** On August 13, 2003, President Bush reported to Congress, "consistent with the War Powers Resolution," that in response to conditions in Liberia, on August 11, 2003, he had authorized about 4,350 U.S. combat-equipped military personnel to enter Liberian territorial waters in support of U.N. and West African States efforts to restore order and provide humanitarian assistance in Liberia.

110. **Anti-terrorist operations.** On September 19, 2003, President Bush reported to Congress "consistent with the War Powers Resolution," that U.S. "combat-equipped and combat support forces" continue to be deployed at a number of locations around the world as part of U.S. anti-terrorism efforts. American forces support anti-terrorism efforts in the Philippines, and maritime interception operations continue on the high seas in the Central, European and Pacific Command areas of responsibility, to "prevent the movement, arming, or financing of international terrorists." He also noted that "U.S. combat equipped and support forces" had been deployed to Georgia and Djibouti to help in enhancing their "counterterrorist capabilities."

111. **Yugoslavia/Kosovo.** On November 14, 2003, the President reported to Congress "consistent with the War Powers Resolution" that the United States was continuing to deploy combat equipped military personnel as part of the NATO-led international security force in Kosovo (KFOR). Currently the United States has approximately 2,100 U.S. military personnel in Kosovo, with additional American military personnel operating out of Macedonia, Albania, and Greece, in support of KFOR operations.

112. **Bosnia.** On January 22, 2004, the President reported to Congress "consistent with the War Powers Resolution" that the United States was continuing to deploy combat equipped military personnel in Bosnia and Herzegovina in support of NATO's Stabilization Force (SFOR) and its peacekeeping efforts in this country. About 1,800 U.S. personnel are participating.

113. **Haiti.** On February 25, 2004, the President reported to Congress "consistent with the War Powers Resolution" that, on February 23, he had sent a combat-equipped "security force" of about"55 U.S. military personnel from the U.S. Joint Forces Command" to Port-au-Prince, Haiti to augment the U.S. Embassy security forces there and to protect American citizens and property in light of the instability created by the armed rebellion in Haiti.

114. **Haiti.** On March 2, 2004, the President reported to Congress "consistent with the War Powers Resolution" that on February 29 he had sent about "200 additional U.S. combat-equipped, military personnel from the U.S. Joint Forces Command" to Port-au-Prince, Haiti for a variety of purposes, including preparing the way for a UN Multinational Interim Force, and otherwise supporting UN Security Council Resolution 1529 (2004).

115. **Anti-terrorist operations.** On March 20, 2004, the President sent to Congress "consistent with the War Powers Resolution," a consolidated report giving details of multiple ongoing United States military deployments and operations "in support of the global war on terrorism (including in Afghanistan)," as well as operations in Bosnia and Herzegovina, Kosovo, and Haiti. In this report, the President noted that U.S. anti-terror related activities were underway in Georgia, Djibouti, Kenya, Ethiopia, Yemen, and Eritrea. He further noted that U.S. combat-equipped military personnel continued to be deployed in Kosovo as part of the NATO-led KFOR (1,900 personnel); in Bosnia and Herzegovina as part of the NATO-led SFOR (about 1,100 personnel); and approximately 1,800 military personnel were deployed in Haiti as part of the U.N. Multinational Interim Force.

War Powers Resolution: Presidential Compliance   119

116. **Anti-terrorist operations.** On November 4, 2004, the President sent to Congress, "consistent with the War Powers Resolution," a consolidated report giving details of multiple ongoing United States military deployments and operations "in support of the global war on terrorism." These deployments, support or military operations include activities in Afghanistan, Djibouti, as well as Kenya, Ethiopia, Eritrea, Bosnia and Herzegovina, and Kosovo. In this report, the President noted that U.S. anti-terror related activities were underway in Djibouti, Kenya, Ethiopia, Yemen, and Eritrea. He further noted that U.S. combat-equipped military personnel continued to be deployed in Kosovo as part of the NATO-led KFOR (1,800 personnel); and in Bosnia and Herzegovina as part of the NATO-led SFOR (about 1,000 personnel). Meanwhile, he stated that the United States continues to deploy more than 135,000 military personnel in Iraq.

117. **Anti-terrorist operations.** On May 20, 2005, the President sent to Congress "consistent with the War Powers Resolution," a consolidated report giving details of multiple ongoing United States military deployments and operations "in support of the global war on terrorism," as well as operations in Iraq, where currently about 139,000 U.S. military personnel are stationed. U.S. forces are also deployed in Kenya, Ethiopia, Yemen, Eritrea, and Djibouti assisting in "enhancing counter-terrorism capabilities" of these nations. The President further noted that U.S. combat-equipped military personnel continued to be deployed in Kosovo as part of the NATO-led KFOR (1,700 personnel). Approximately235 U.S. personnel are also deployed in Bosnia and Herzegovina as part of the NATO Headquarters-Sarajevo who assist in defense reform and perform operational tasks, such as counter-terrorism and supporting the International Criminal Court for the Former Yugoslavia.

118. **Anti-terrorist operations.** On December 7, 2005, the President sent to Congress "consistent" with the War Powers Resolution, a consolidated report giving details of multiple ongoing United States military deployments and operations "in support of the global war on terrorism," and in support of the Multinational Force in Iraq, where about 160, 000 U.S. military personnel are deployed. U.S. forces are also deployed in the Horn of Africa region — Kenya, Ethiopia, Yemen, and Djibouti — assisting in "enhancing counter-terrorism

capabilities" of these nations. The President further noted that U.S. combat-equipped military personnel continued to be deployed in Kosovo as part of the NATO-led KFOR (1,700 personnel). Approximately 220 U.S. personnel are also deployed in Bosnia and Herzegovina as part of the NATO Headquarters-Sarajevo who assist in defense reform and perform operational tasks, such as "counter-terrorism and supporting the International Criminal Court for the Former Yugoslavia."

119. **Anti-terrorist operations.** On June 15, 2006, the President sent to Congress "consistent" with the War Powers Resolution, a consolidated report giving details of multiple ongoing United States military deployments and operations "in support of the war on terror," and in Kosovo, Bosnia and Herzegovina, and as part of the Multinational Force (MNF) in Iraq. Presently, about 131, 000 military personnel were deployed in Iraq. U.S. forces were also deployed in the Horn of Africa region, and in Djibouti to support necessary operations against al-Qaida and other international terrorists operating in the region. U.S. military personnel continue to support the NATO-led Kosovo Force (KFOR). The current U.S. contribution to KFOR is about 1,700 military personnel. The NATO Headquarters-Sarajevo was established in November 22, 2004 as a successor to its stabilization operations in Bosnia-Herzegovina to continue to assist in implementing the peace agreement. Approximately 250 U.S. personnel are assigned to the NATO Headquarters-Sarajevo who assist in defense reform and perform operational tasks, such as "counter-terrorism and supporting the International Criminal Court for the Former Yugoslavia."

120. **Lebanon.** On July 18, 2006, the President reported to Congress "consistent" with the War Powers Resolution, that in response to the security threat posed in Lebanon to U.S. Embassy personnel and citizens and designated third country personnel," he had deployed combat-equipped military helicopters and military personnel to Beirut to assist in the departure of the persons under threat from Lebanon. The President noted that additional combat-equipped U.S. military forces may be deployed "to Lebanon, Cyprus and other locations, as necessary." to assist further departures of persons from Lebanon and to provide security. He further stated that once the threat to U.S.

citizens and property has ended, the U.S. military forces would redeploy.

121. **Anti-terrorist operations.** On December 15, 2006, the President sent to Congress "consistent" with the War Powers Resolution, a consolidated report giving details of multiple ongoing United States military deployments and operations "in support of the war on terror," in Kosovo, Bosnia and Herzegovina, and as part of the Multinational Force (MNF) in Iraq. Presently, about 134, 000 military personnel are deployed in Iraq. U.S. forces were also deployed in the Horn of Africa region, and in Djibouti to support necessary operations against al-Qaida and other international terrorists operating in the region, including Yemen. U.S. military personnel continue to support the NATO-led Kosovo Force (KFOR). The current U.S. contribution to KFOR is about 1,700 military personnel. The NATO Headquarters-Sarajevo was established in November 22, 2004 as a successor to its stabilization operations in Bosnia-Herzegovinato continue to assist in implementing the peace agreement. Approximately 100 U.S. personnel are assigned to the NATO Headquarters-Sarajevo who assist in defense reform and perform operational tasks, such as "counter-terrorism and supporting the International Criminal Court for the Former Yugoslavia."

122. **Anti-terrorist operations.** On June 15, 2007, the President sent to Congress, "consistent" with the War Powers Resolution, a consolidated report giving details of ongoing U.S. military deployments and operations "in support of the war on terror,"and in support of the NATO-led Kosovo Force (KFOR). The President reported that various U.S. "combat-equipped and combat-support forces" were deployed to "a number of locations in the Central, Pacific, European (KFOR), and Southern Command areas of operation" and were engaged in combat operations against al-Qaida terrorists and their supporters. The United States is currently "pursuing and engaging remnant al-Qaida and Taliban fighters in Afghanistan." U.S. forces in Afghanistan currently total approximately 25,945. Of this total, "approximately 14,340 are assigned to the International Security Assistance Force (ISAF) in Afghanistan." The U.S. military continues to support peacekeeping operations in Kosovo, specifically the NATO-led Kosovo Force

(KFOR). Currently, the U.S. contribution to KFOR in Kosovo is approximately 1,584 military personnel.

123. **Anti-terrorist operations.** On December 14, 2007, the President sent to Congress, "consistent with the War Powers Resolution," a consolidated report givingdetails of ongoing U.S. military deployments and operations "in support of the war on terror,"and in support of the NATO-led Kosovo Force (KFOR). The President reported that various U.S. "combat-equipped and combat-support forces" were deployed to "a number of locations in the Central, Pacific, European, and Southern Command areas of operation" and were engaged in combat operations against al-Qaida terrorists and their supporters. The United States is currently "pursuing and engaging remnant al-Qaida and Taliban fighters in Afghanistan." U.S. forces in Afghanistan currently total approximately 25,900. Of this total, "approximately 15,180 are assigned to the International Security Assistance Force (ISAF) in Afghanistan." The U.S. military continues to support peacekeeping operations in Kosovo, specifically the NATO-led Kosovo Force (KFOR). Currently, the U.S. contribution to KFOR in Kosovo is approximately1,498 military personnel.

APPENDIX B. INSTANCES NOT FORMALLY REPORTED TO THE CONGRESS UNDER THE WAR POWERS RESOLUTION

In some instances where U.S. Armed Forces have been deployed in potentially hostile situations abroad, Presidents did not submit reports to Congress under the War Powers Resolution and the question of whether a report was required could be raised. Representative examples of these instances since 1973 include:[106]

- evacuation of civilians from Cyprus in 1974
- evacuation of civilians from Lebanon in 1976
- Korean DMZ tree-cutting incident of 1976
- transport of European troops to Zaire in 1978
- dispatch of additional military advisers to El Salvador in 1981
- shooting down of two Libyan jets over the Gulf of Sidra on August 19, 1981, after one had fired a heat-seeking missile

- the use of training forces in Honduras after 1983
- dispatch of AWACS to Egypt after a Libyan plane bombed a city in Sudan March 18, 1983
- shooting down of two Iranian fighter planes over Persian Gulf on June 5, 1984, by Saudi Arabian jet fighter planes aided by intelligence from a U.S. AWACS
- interception by U.S. Navy pilots on October 10, 1985, of an Egyptian airliner carrying hijackers of the Italian cruise ship *Achille Lauro*
- use of U.S. Army personnel and aircraft in Bolivia for anti-drug assistance on July 14, 1986
- buildup of fleet in Persian Gulf area in 1987
- force augmentations in Panama in 1988 and 1989
- shooting down 2 Libyan jet fighters over the Mediterranean Sea on January 4, 1989
- dispatch of military advisers and Special Forces teams to Colombia, Bolivia, and Peru, in the Andean initiative, announced September 5, 1989, to help those nations combat illicit drug traffickers
- transport of Belgian troops and equipment into Zaire September 25-27, 1991
- evacuation of non-essential U.S. government workers and families from Sierra Leone, May 3, 1992
- a bombing campaign against Iraq, termed Operation Desert Fox, aimed at destroying Iraqi industrial facilities deemed capable of producing weapons of mass destruction, as well as other Iraqi military and security targets, December 16-23, 1998.

APPENDIX C. TEXT OF THE WAR POWERS RESOLUTION

War Powers Resolution[107]

Public Law 93-148 [H.J.Res. 542], 87 Stat. 555, passed over President's veto November 7, 1973

JOINT RESOLUTION Concerning the war powers of Congress and the President.

Resolved by the Senate and House of Representatives of the United States of America in Congress assembled,

Short Title

SECTION 1. This joint resolution may be cited as the "War Powers Resolution".

Purpose and Policy

SEC. 2.[108]

(a) It is the purpose of this joint resolution to fulfill the intent of the framers of the Constitution of the United States and insure that the collective judgment of both the Congress and the President will apply to the introduction of United States Armed Forces into hostilities, or into situations where imminent involvement in hostilities is clearly indicated by the circumstances, and to the continued use of such forces in hostilities or in such situations.

(b) Under article I, section 8, of the Constitution, it is specifically provided that the Congress shall have the power to make all laws necessary and proper for carrying into execution, not only its own powers but also all other powers vested by the Constitution in the Government of the United States, or in any department or officer thereof.

(c) The constitutional powers of the President as Commander-in-Chief to introduce United States Armed Forces into hostilities, or into situations where imminent involvement in hostilities is clearly indicated by the circumstances, are exercised only pursuant to (1) a declaration of war, (2) specific statutory authorization, or (3) a national emergency created by attack upon the United States, its territories or possessions, or its armed forces.

Consultation

SEC. 3.[109] The President in every possible instance shall consult with Congress before introducing United States Armed Forces into hostilities or into situations where imminent involvement in hostilities is clearly indicated by the circumstances, and after every such introduction shall consult regularly with the Congress until United States Armed Forces are no longer engaged in hostilities or have been removed from such situations.

Reporting

SEC. 4.[110]
(a) In the absence of a declaration of war, in any case in which United States Armed Forces are introduced —
(1) into hostilities or into situations where imminent involvement in hostilities is clearly indicated by the circumstances;
(2) into the territory, airspace, or waters of a foreign nation, while equipped for combat, except for deployments which relate solely to supply, replacement, repair, or training of such forces; or
(3) in numbers which substantially enlarge United States Armed Forces equipped for combat already located in a foreign nation; the President shall submit within 48 hours to the Speaker of the House of Representatives and to the President pro tempore of the Senate a report, in writing, setting forth —
(A) the circumstances necessitating the introduction of United States Armed Forces;
(B) the constitutional and legislative authority under which such introduction took place; and
(C) the estimated scope and duration of the hostilities or involvement.
(b) The President shall provide such other information as the Congress may request in the fulfillment of its constitutional responsibilities with respect to committing the Nation to war and to the use of United States Armed Forces abroad.
(c) Whenever United States Armed Forcesareintroducedinto hostilities or into any situation described in subsection (a) of this section, the President shall, so long as such armed forces continue to be engaged in such hostilities or situation, report to the Congress periodically on the status of such hostilities or situation as well as on the scope and duration of such hostilities or situation, but in no event shall he report to the Congress less often than once every six months.

Congressional Action

SEC. 5.[111]

(a) Each report submitted pursuant to section 4(a)(1) shall be transmitted to the Speaker of the House of Representatives and to the President pro tempore of the Senate on the same calendar day. Each report so transmitted shall be referred to the Committee on Foreign Affairs[112] of the House of Representatives and to the Committee on Foreign Relations of the Senate for appropriate action. If, when the report is transmitted, the Congress has adjourned sine die or has adjourned for any period in excess of three calendar days, the Speaker of the House of Representatives and the President pro tempore of the Senate, if they deem it advisable(or if petitioned by at least 30 percent of the membership of their respective Houses) shall jointly request the President to convene Congress in order that it may consider the report and take appropriate action pursuant to this section.

(b) Within sixty calendar days after a report is submitted or is required to be submitted pursuant to section 4(a)(1), whichever is earlier, the President shall terminate any use of United States Armed Forces with respect to which such report was submitted (or required to besubmitted), unless the Congress (1) has declared war or has enacted a specific authorization for such use of United States Armed Forces, (2) has extended by law such sixty-day period, or (3) is physically unable to meet as a result of an armed attack upon the United States. Such sixty-day period shall be extended for not more than an additional thirty days if the President determines and certifies to the Congress in writing that unavoidable military necessity respecting the safetyof United States Armed Forces requires the continued use of such armed forces in the course of bringing about a prompt removal of such forces.

(c) Notwithstanding subsection (b), atany time that United States Armed Forces are engaged in hostilities outside the territory of theUnited States, its possessions and territories without a declaration of war or specific statutory authorization, such forces shall be removed bythe President if the Congress so directs by concurrent resolution.

Congressional Priority Procedures for Joint Resolution or Bill

SEC. 6.[113]

(a) Any joint resolution or bill introduced pursuant to section 5(b) at least thirty calendar days before the expiration of the sixty-day period specified in such section, shall be referred to the Committee on Foreign Affairs of the House of Representatives or the Committee on Foreign Relations of the Senate, as the case may be, and such committee shall report one such joint resolution or bill, together with its recommendations, not later than twenty-four calendar days before the expiration of the sixty-day period specified in such section, unless such House shall otherwise determine by the yeas and nays.

(b) Any joint resolution or bill so reported shall become the pending business of the House in question (in thecaseof theSenatethetime for debate shall be equally divided between the proponents and the opponents), and shall be voted on within three calendar days thereafter, unless such House shall otherwise determine by yeas and nays.

(c) Such a joint resolution or bill passed by one House shall be referred to the committee of the other House named in subsection (a) and shall be reported out not later than fourteen calendar days before the expiration of the sixty-day period specified in section 5(b). The joint resolution or bill so reported shall become the pending business of the House in question and shall be voted on within three calendar days after it has been reported, unless such House shall otherwise determine by yeas and nays.

(d) In the case of any disagreement between the two Houses of Congress with respect to a joint resolution or bill passed by both Houses, conferees shall be promptly appointed and the committee of conference shall make and file a report with respect to such resolution or bill not later than four calendar days before the expiration of the sixty-day period specified in section 5(b). In the event the conferees are unable to agree within 48 hours, they shall report back to their respective House in disagreement. Notwithstanding any rule in either House concerning the printing of conference reports in the Record or concerning any delay in the consideration of such reports, such report shall be acted on by both Houses not later than the expiration of such sixty-day period.

Congressional Priority Procedures for Concurrent Resolution

Sec. 7.[114]

(a) Any concurrent resolution introduced pursuantto section 5(c) shall be referred to the Committee on Foreign Affairs of the House of Representatives or the Committee on Foreign Relations of the Senate, as the case may be, and one such concurrent resolution shall be reported out by such committee together with its recommendations within fifteen calendar days, unless such House shall otherwise determine by the yeas and nays.

(b) Any concurrent resolution so reported shall become the pending business of the House in question (in the case of the Senate the time for debate shall be equally divided between the proponents and the opponents) and shall be voted on within three calendar days thereafter, unless such House shall otherwise determine by yeas and nays.

(c) Such a concurrent resolution passed by one House shall be referred to the committee of the other House named in subsection (a) and shall be reported out by such committee together with its recommendations within fifteen calendar days and shall thereupon become the pending business of such House and shall be voted upon within three calendar days, unless such House shall otherwise determine by yeas and nays.

(d) In the case of any disagreement between the two Houses of Congress with respect to a concurrent resolution passed byboth Houses, conferees shall be promptly appointed and the committee of conference shall make and file a report with respect to such concurrent resolution within six calendar days after the legislation is referred to the committee of conference. Notwithstandinganyrulein either House concerning the printing of conference reports in the Record or concerning any delay in the consideration of such reports, such report shall be acted on by both Houses not later than six calendar days after the conference report is filed. In the event the conferees are unable to agree within 48 hours, they shall report back to their respective Houses in disagreement.

Interpretation of Joint Resolution

SEC. 8.[115]

(a) Authority to introduce United States Armed Forces into hostilities or into situations wherein involvement in hostilities is clearly indicated by the circumstances shall not be inferred —

(1) from any provision of law (whether or not in effect before the date of the enactment of this joint resolution), including any provision contained in any appropriation Act, unless such provision specifically authorizes the introduction of United States Armed Forces into hostilities or into such situations and states that it is intended to constitute specific statutory authorization within the meaning of this joint resolution; or

(2) from any treaty heretofore or hereafter ratified unless such treaty is implemented by legislation specifically authorizing the introduction of United States Armed Forces into hostilities or into such situations and stating that it is intended to constitute specific statutory authorization within the meaning of this joint resolution.

(b) Nothing in this joint resolution shall be construed to require any further specific statutory authorization to permit members of United States Armed Forces to participate jointly with members of the armed forces of one or more foreign countries in the headquarters operations of high-level military commands which were established prior to the date of enactment of this joint resolution and pursuant to the United Nations Charter or any treaty ratified by the United States prior to such date.

(c) For purposes of this joint resolution, the term "introduction of United States Armed Forces" includes the assignment of members of such armed forces to command, coordinate, participate in the movement of, or accompany the regular or irregular military forces of any foreign country or government when such military forces are engaged, or there exists an imminent threat that such forces will become engaged, in hostilities.

(d) Nothing in this joint resolution —

(1) is intended to alter the constitutional authority of the Congress or of the President, or the provisions of existing treaties; or

(2) shall be construed as granting any authority to the President with respect to the introduction of United States Armed Forces into hostilities or into situations wherein involvement in hostilities is clearly indicated by the circumstances which authority he would not have had in the absence of this joint resolution.

Separability Clause

SEC. 9.[116] If any provision of this joint resolution or the application thereof to any person or circumstances is held invalid, the remainder of the joint resolution and the application of such provision to any other person or circumstance shall not be affected thereby.

Effective Date

Sec. 10.[117] This joint resolution shall take effect on the date of its enactment.

End Notes

[1] U.S. Congress. H.Rept. 93-287, p. 6.
[2] U.S. Congress. H.Rept. 93-287, p. 7.
[3] U.S. Congress. H.Rept. 93-287, p. 7.
[4] U.S. Congress. H.Rept. 93-287, p. 8.
[5] U.S. Congress. H.Rept. 93-547, p. 8.
[6] P.L. 88-408, approved August 10, 1964; repealed in 1971 by P.L. 91-672.
[7] U.S. Congress. S.Rept. 93-220, p. 24.
[8] United States. President (Nixon). Message vetoing House Joint Resolution 542, A Joint Resolution Concerning the War Powers of Congress and the President. October 24, 1973. H.Doc. 93-171.
[9] U.S. Congress. House. Committee on International Relations. War Powers: A Test of Compliance relative to the Danang Sealift, the Evacuation of Phnom Penh, the Evacuation of Saigon, and the Mayaguez Incident. Hearings, May 7 and June 4, 1975. Washington, U.S. Govt. Printing Off., 1975. p. 69.
[10] 462 U.S. 919 (1983).
[11] Federal Trade Commission Improvements Act of 1980.
[12] Process Gas Consumers Group v. Consumer Energy Council, 463 U.S. 1216 (1983).
[13] Celada, Raymond. J. Effect of the Legislative Veto Decision on the Two-House Disapproval Mechanism to Terminate U.S. Involvement in Hostilities Pursuant to Unilateral Presidential Action. CRS Report, August 24, 1983.
[14] Gressman, Prof. Eugene. In U.S. Congress. House. Committee on Foreign Affairs. The U.S. Supreme Court Decision Concerning the Legislative Veto. Hearings, July 19, 20, and 21, 1983. 98th Congress, 1st sess. Washington, U.S. GPO, 1983, p. 155-157. Buchanan, G. Sidney. In Defense of the War Powers Resolution: Chadha Does Not Apply. Houston Law Review, Vol. 22, p. 1155; Ely, John Hart. Suppose Congress Wanted a War Powers Act that Worked. Columbia Law Review, Vol. 88, p. 1379 (see p. 1395-1398).
[15] U.S. Congress. House. Committee on Foreign Affairs. U.S. Supreme Court Decision Concerning the Legislative Veto, Hearings, p. 52.
[16] P.L. 94-329, signed June 30, 1976.

War Powers Resolution: Presidential Compliance   131

[17] Senate amendment to S. 1324. Section 1013, State Department Authorization Act for FY1984, P.L. 98-164, approved November 22, 1983. Codified at 50 U.S.C. , sect.1546a (1994).

[18] H.Rept. 103-329, November 5, 1993, p. 2. See below for further discussion of the Somalia case.

[19] The Senate bill had a time limit of 30 days. U.S. Congress. Senate. Committee on Foreign Relations. War Powers. Report to accompany S. 440. S.Rept. 93-220, 93d Congress, 1st Session. p. 28.

[20] Sofaer, Abraham D. Prepared statement in: U.S. Congress. Senate. Committee on Foreign Relations. The War Power After 200 Years: Congress and the President at a Constitutional Impasse. Hearings before the Special Subcommittee on War Powers. July 13-September 29, 1988. S.Hrng. 100-1012. p. 1059.

[21] Appendix A lists in chronological order all reports to Congress related to the War Powers Resolution from the first in 1975 through 2003. Appendix B lists representative instances of the deployment to or use of armed forces in potentially hostile situations which were not reported under the Resolution. Appendix C gives the complete text of the War Powers Resolution.

[22] U.S. Congress. House. Committee on International Relations. War Powers: A Test of Compliance Relative to the Danang Sealift, the Evacuation of Phnom Penh, the Evacuation of Saigon, and the Mayaguez Incident. Hearings, May 7 and June 4, 1975. Washington, U.S. Govt. Print. Off., 1975. P. 3.

[23] U.S. Congress. Senate. Committee on Foreign Relations. The situation in Iran. Hearing, 96th Congress, 2nd session. May 8, 1980. Washington, U.S. Govt. Print. Off., 1980. P. iii.

[24] Congressional Record, March 5, 1981, V. 127, p. 3743.

[25] *Crockett v. Reagan*, 558 F. Supp. 893 (D.D.C. 1982).

[26] 720 F. 2d 1355 (D.C.Cir. 1983), cert. denied, 467 U.S. 1251 (1984).

[27] On March 8, 1982, Senator Robert Byrd introduced the War Powers Resolution Amendment of 1982 (S. 2179) specifically providing that U.S. armed forces shall not be introduced into El Salvador for combat unless (1) the Congress has declared war or specifically authorized such use; or (2) such introduction was necessary to meet a clear and present danger of attack on the United States or to provide immediate evacuation of U.S. citizens. Similar bills were introduced in the House, e.g. H.R. 1619 and H.R. 1777 in the 98th Congress.

[28] H.Con.Res. 87, 97th Congress.

[29] Report on S.J.Res. 158, Sec. III, S.Rept. 97-470, June 9, 1982.

[30] *Congressional Record*, House, July 26, 1983, pp. 20924-20925.

[31] The initial statutory restriction was contained in the Continuing Appropriations Resolution for 1983, P.L. 97-377. This was followed by a $24 million ceiling on intelligence agency support in FY1984.

[32] Sec. 1451 of P.L.99-145, approved November 8, 1985. A similar provision was contained in the defense authorization for 1988-1989, sec.1405 of P.L.100-180, approved December 4, 1987.

[33] Continuing Appropriations Resolution, P. L. 99-591, approved October 30, 1986. Continued in P.L. 100-202, approved December 22, 1987.

[34] P.L. 98-119, approved October 12, 1983.

[35] P.L. 98-43, approved June 27, 1983.

[36] P.L. 98-119, signed October 12, 1983.

[37] U.S. Congress. H.Rept. 98-566 on H.J.Res. 308; Senate amendment numbered 3. Congressional Record November 17, 1983, p. H10189.

[38] *Conyers v. Reagan*, 578 F. Supp. 323 (D.D.C. 1984).

[39] *Conyers v. Reagan*, 765 F.2d 1124 (D.C. Cir. 1985).

[40] S.J.Res. 340, introduced May 8, 1986. The bill was not acted upon, but the proposal was later incorporated in other proposed amendments. See below, section on amendments.

[41] S. 2335 and H.R. 4611, Anti-Terrorism Act of 1986, introduced April 17, 1986. Not acted upon.

[42] For the reports, see list above under section on reporting requirements.

[43] Questions submitted to Department of State and responses thereto, March 30, 1988, in War Powers Resolution, Relevant Documents, Correspondence, Reports, p. 97-99.

[44] Bills to this effect in the House included H.J.Res. 387, introduced October 22, 1987, which also authorized the continued presence of U.S. forces in the Gulf.

[45] Byrd-Warner amendment to S.J.Res. 194, adopted by Senate October 21, 1987.

[46] Lowry v. Reagan, 676 F. Supp. 333 (D.D.C. 1987). See also CRS Report RL30352, *War Powers Litigation Since the Enactment of the War Powers Resolution*, by David M. Ackerman.

[47] Weinberger, Caspar W. Secretary of Defense. A Report to the Congress on Security Arrangements in the Persian Gulf. June 15, 1987, p.14.

[48] When asked about abiding by the War Powers Resolution, **President Reagan said "we are complying with a part of that act,** although we do not call it that. But we have been consulting the Congress, **reporting to them and telling them what we're doing, and in advance..." Press conference of October 22,1987.** *The New York Times*, October 23, 1987, p. A8.

[49] P.L. 101-162, signed November 21, 1989.

[50] Amendments to National Drug Control Strategy bill, S. 1711, October 5, 1989.

[51] In that case, the Soviet Union had absented itself from the Council temporarily, and the Security Council requested members to supply the Republic of Korea with sufficient military assistance to repel the invasion of North Korea. President Truman ordered U.S. air, naval, and ground forces to Korea to repel the attack without authorization from Congress. **Senator Robert Taft complained on January 5, 1951, "The President simply usurped authority** in violation of the laws and the Constitution, when he sent troops to Korea to carry out the resolution of the United Nations in an undeclared war."

[52] Such a statement was made in the Authorization for Use of Military Force against Iraq Resolution, P.L. 102-1, signed January 14, 1991, and in S.J.Res. 45, authorizing the use of force in Somalia for one year, as passed by the Senate on February 4, 1993, and amended by the House on May 25, 1993; a conference was not held.

[53] U.S. Congress. Senate. Committee on Foreign Relations. War Powers; report to accompany S. 440. June 14, 1973. S.Rept. 93-220.

[54] Sec.8153, Department of Defense Appropriation Act for FY1994, H.R. 3116, P.L. 103-139, signed November 11, 1993.

[55] Sec. 1502 (11), Defense Authorization Act for FY1994, P.L. 103-160, signed November 30, 1993.

[56] For background see CRS Report RL33557, *Peacekeeping and Related Stability Operations: Issues of U.S. Military Involvement*, by Nina M. Serafino.

[57] On August 17, 1990, Acting Secretary of State Robert M. Kimmitt sent a formal letter to Congress (not mentioning the War Powers Resolution**) stating, "It is not our intention or expectation** that the use of force will be required to carry out these operations. However, if other means of enforcement fail, necessary and proportionate force will be employed to deny passage to ships that are in violation of these sanctions."

[58] Dellums v. Bush, 752 F. Supp. 1141 (D.D.C. 1990).

[59] Statement by Secretary of Defense Richard Cheney. U.S. Congress. Senate. Committee on Armed Services. Crisis in the Persian Gulf Region: U.S. Policy Options and Implications. September 11-December 3, 1990, S.Hrg. 101-1071, pp. 701-2.

[60] Weekly Compilation of Presidential Documents. January 14, 1991. Vol. 27, No. 2, pp.17-18; pp. 24-25.

[61] The House passed H.J.Res. 77 by a vote of 250 to 183. The Senate passed S.J.Res. 2 and then considered H.J.Res. 77 as passed. The Senate vote was 52 to 47. The bill became P.L. 102-1, signed January 14, 1991. On January 12, to emphasize the congressional power to declare war, the House also adopted by a vote of 302 to 131 H.Con.Res. 32 expressing the sense

War Powers Resolution: Presidential Compliance   133

that Congress must approve any offensive military actions against Iraq; the Senate did not act on the measure.

[62] Weekly Compilation of Presidential Documents. January 21, 1991. Vol. 27, No. 3, pp.48-49. Subsequently, on June 20,1992, during remarks to the Texas State Republican Convention in Dallas, Texas, President Bush said: "Some people say, why can't you bring the same kind of purpose and success to the domestic scene as you did in Desert Shield and Desert Storm? And the answer is: I didn't have to get permission from some old goat in the United States Congress to kick Saddam Hussein out of Kuwait. That's the reason." Weekly Compilation of Presidential Documents. June 29, 1992. Vol. 28, No. 26, pp.1120-1121.

[63] Section 1512, P.L. 103-160, signed November 30, 1993.

[64] Sec. 8151 of P.L. 103-139, signed November 11, 1993.

[65] For additional discussion of H.Con.Res. 170, see section on Legislative Veto, above.

[66] The name of this area is in dispute. The provisional name, which is used for its designation as a member of the United Nations, is "The Former Yugoslav Republic of Macedonia." This report uses the term "Macedonia" without prejudice.

[67] For additional background see CRS Report RS22324, *Bosnia: Overview of Current Issues*, by Julie Kim.

[68] For additional background see CRS Report RL32392, *Bosnia and Herzegovina: Issues for U.S. Policy*, by Steven Woehrel, and CRS Report RL32282, *Bosnia and Kosovo: U.S. Military Operations*, by Steve Bowman.

[69] Campbell v. Clinton. Civil Action No. 99-1072.

[70] The McCain joint resolution (S.J.Res. 20) authorizing Presidential action in Yugoslavia was forced to the Senate floor by the Senator's use of the expedited procedures set out in section 6 of the War Powers Resolution for consideration of such resolutions. See debate and discussion in U.S. Congressional Record, Senate, May 3, 1999, pp. S4514-S4572; and May 4, 1999, pp. S4611-S4616 [daily edition].

[71] U.S. Congressional Record, Senate, May 24, 1999, pp. S5809-S5840 [daily edition].

[72] U.S. Congressional Record, Senate, May 26, 1999, pp. S6034-S6040 [daily edition].

[73] Seethe June 8, 1999 decision of Judge Friedman of the U.S. District Court for the District of Columbia at 52 F. Supp. 2d 34 (1999).

[74] Campbell v. Clinton, 203 F.3d 19 (D.C. Cir. 2000).

[75] Campbell v. Clinton, *cert. denied*, 531 U.S.815 October 2, 2000).

[76] For detailed discussion of major issues see CRS Report RL31053, *Kosovo and U.S. Policy: Background and Current Issues*, by Julie Kim and Steven J. Woehrel, and CRS Report RL30352, *War Powers Litigation Since the Enactment of the War Powers Resolution*, by David M. Ackerman.

[77] For further information on Haiti, see Haiti: Issues for Congress, CRS Report RL32294.

[78] Presidential statement of September 12, 2001. Office of the White House Press Secretary. See White House website at [http://whitehouse.gov/news/releases].

[79] For background on discussions regardingthe resolution see: Washington Post, September 13, 2001, p.A3; CQ Daily Monitor, September 13, 2001, p.2, 6; CQ Daily Monitor, September 14, 2001, p.2; Washington Post, September 14, 2001, p. A30; The New York Times, September 14, 2001, p.A19; Roll Call, September 20, 2001, p.17. The debate on S. J. Res. 23 is found in U.S. Congress. Congressional Record, 107th Congress, 1st session, pp.S9416-S9421 (Senate); H5638-H5683 [daily edition].

[80] P.L. 107-40 (September 18, 2001); 115 Stat. 224.

[81] For detailed legislative history of P.L. 107-40 see CRS Report RS22357, *Authorization For Use of Military Force in Response to the 9/11 Attacks (P.L. 107-40): Legislative History*, by Richard F. Grimmett.

[82] Statement of the President on September 18, 2001. President Signs Authorization for Use of Military Force bill. Office of the White House Press Secretary. September 18, 2001. See White House website at [http://whitehouse.gov/news/releases].

[83] See the White House website for comments by the President to the Congressional leaders and to the U.N. under news (September) at [http://www.whitehouse.gov/news/releases/2002/09/]

[84] P.L. 107-243; 116 Stat. 1498. For a detailed side-by-side comparison of the House and Senate versions of the authorization of force against Iraq legislation and proposed amendments *see* CRS Report RL31596, *Authorization of Use of U.S. Armed Forces Against Iraq: Side-by-Side Comparison of Selected Legislative Proposals*, by Dianne E. Rennack.

[85] For text of President Bush's signing statement for H.J.Res. 114 see the State Department's Washington File entry at [http://usinfo.state.gov/topical/pol/usandun/02101606.htm]

[86] Fascell, Representative Dante B. Testimony. U.S. Congress. Senate. Committee on Foreign Relations. The War Powers after 200 years: Congress and the President at Constitutional Impasse. Hearings, July 13 - September 29, 1988. P. 11.

[87] Examples of bills to repeal the War Powers Resolution include S. 2030 introduced by Senator Barry Goldwater on October 31, 1983, H.R. 2525, introduced by Representative Robert Dornan on May 27, 1987 and S. 5, introduced by Senator Robert Dole on January 4, 1995. See also the most recent major legislative floor debate on repeal of the War Powers Resolution, held on June 7, 1995. This debate centered on an amendment to H.R. 1561, offered by Representative HenryHyde, which would haverepealed most of the key elements of the War Powers Resolution. The amendment was defeated by a vote of 217-201. Congressional Record, June 7, 1995, pp. H5655-H5674[daily edition].

[88] Congressional Record, July 12, 1983, p. S9670.

[89] A broad-gauged proposal reflective of this view is S. 564, Use of Force Act, introduced by Senator Biden on March 15, 1995.

[90] S.J.Res. 323, introduced by Senators Byrd, Warner, and Nunn, May 19, 1988. On September 29, 1983, Senators Cranston, Eagleton, and Stennis introduced an amendment to this effect that had been proposed in the Senate Foreign Relations in July 1977 and known as Committee Print No. 2, July 1, 1977. In U.S. Congress. Senate. Committee on Foreign Relations. War Powers. Hearings, July 13,14 and 15, 1977. Wash., GPO, 1977. P.338. For a review of the use of funding cutoffs by Congress since 1970 see CRS Report RS20775, *Congressional Use of Funding Cutoffs Since 1970 Involving U.S. Military Forces and Overseas Deployments*, by Richard F. Grimmett.,and CRS Report RL33837, *Congressional Authority to Limit U.S. Military Operations in Iraq*, by Jennifer K. Elsea, Michael John Garcia, and Thomas J. Nicola.

[91] See Krotoski, Mark L. Essential Elements of Reform of the War Powers Resolution. Santa Clara Law Review. Vol. 28, Summer 1989, p. 609-750.

[92] S.J.Res. 323, introduced May 19, 1988.

[93] Fascell, Representative Dante. Testimony before Foreign Relations Committee, July 13, 1988.

[94] Strengthening Executive-Legislative Consultation on Foreign Policy. Foreign Affairs Committee Print, October 1983, p. 67.

[95] H.J.Res. 95, War Powers Amendments of 1995, introduced by Representative DeFazio, June 16, 1995.

[96] H.R. 3912, Introduced by Representative Lungren, February 4, 1988. Biden, Joseph R. Jr. and John B. Ritch. The War Power at a Constitutional Impasse: a "Joint Decision" Solution. Georgetown Law Journal, Vol. 77:367.

[97] Two of the reports did not mention the War Powers Resolution but met the basic requirement of reporting specified deployments or uses of forces. For the text of the reports until April 12, 1994, and other key documents and correspondence see U.S. Congress. House. Committee on Foreign Affairs. Subcommittee on International Security, International Organizations and Human Rights. The War Powers Resolution, Relevant Documents, Reports, Correspondence. Committee Print., 103rd Congress, second session, May 1994. 267 p.

[98] U.S. Congress. House. Committee on International Relations. War Powers: A test of compliance relative to the Danang sealift, the evacuation of Phnom Penh, the evacuation of

Saigon, and the Mayaguez incident. Hearings, May 7 and June 4, 1975. Washington, U.S. Govt. Printing Off., 1975. P. 3.

[99] Ibid., p. 6.

[100] Ibid., p. 78.

[101] Oberdorfer, Don and John M. Goshko. Peace-keeping Force. Washington Post, July 7, 1982, p. 1.

[102] Gwetzman, Bernard. U.S. To Send Back Marines to Beirut. New York Times, September 21, 1982, p. 1.

[103] U.S. Declares Goal in to Protect Americans and Restore Order. Washington Post, October 26, 1983. P. A7.

[104] Earlier, on September 21, 1987, Secretary of State George P. Shultz submitted a report concerning the Iraqi aircraft missile attack on the U.S.S. Stark in the Persian Gulf similar to reports in this list submitted by Presidents. The report did not mention the War Powers Resolution but said the U.S. presence had been maintained in the Gulf pursuant to the authority of the President as Commander-in-Chief.

[105] See footnote 66 above discussing Macedonia.

[106] The list does not include military assistance or training operations generally considered routine, forces dispatched for humanitarian reasons such as disaster relief, or covert actions. War powers questions have not been raised about U.S. armed forces dispatched for humanitarian aid in peaceful situations, such as 8,000 marines and sailors sent to Bangladesh on May 12, 1991, to provide disaster relief after a cyclone. The War Powers Resolution applies only to the introduction of forces into situations of hostilities or imminent hostilities and to forces equipped for combat.

[107] As presented in *Legislation on Foreign Relations*, volume II, Joint Committee Print of the House Committee on International Relations and Senate Committee on Foreign Relations.

[108] 50 U.S.C. 1541.

See also the authorization for participation in a multinational force in Lebanon, 1983 (Public Law 98-119; 97 Stat. 805).

See also the sense of Congress regarding the possible introduction of U.S. Armed Forces into El Salvador, 1984 (Public Law 98-473; 98 Stat. 1904, 1942).

See also the introduction of U.S. Armed Forces into Central America for combat, 1984 (sec. 310 of Public Law 98-525; 98 Stat. 2516).

See also the authorization for use of U.S. military force against Iraq, 1991 (Public Law 102-1; 105 Stat. 3).

See also Congressional findings and conditional authorization for use of U.S. military force in Somalia, 1993 (sec. 8151 of Public Law 103-139; 107 Stat. 1475), and the sense of the Congress and a statement of Congressional policy on U.S. armed forces in Somalia, 1993 (sec. 1512 of Public Law 103-160; 107 Stat. 1840).

See also the Joint Resolution regarding U.S. policy toward Haiti, 1994 (Public Law 103-423; 108 Stat. 4358).

See also the limitation on deployment of U.S. Armed Forces in Haiti during Fiscal Year 2000 and congressional notification of deployments, 1999 (sec. 1232 of Public Law 106-65, 113 Stat. 788).

See also the authorization for use of military force in the global war against terrorism, 2001 (Public Law 107-40; 115 Stat. 224).

See also the authorization for use of militaryforce against Iraq, 2002 (Public Law107243; 116 Stat. 1498).

[109] 50 U.S.C. 1542.

[110] 50 U.S.C. 1543.

[111] 50 U.S.C. 1544. Consider also sec. 1013 of the Department of State Authorization Act, Fiscal Years 1984 and 1985 (Public Law 98-164; 97 Stat. 1062; 50 U.S.C. 1546a) which provides: "EXPEDITED PROCEDURES FOR CERTAIN JOINT RESOLUTION AND BILLS "SEC. 1013. Any joint resolution or bill introduced in either House which requires the

removal of United States Armed Forces engaged in hostilities outside the territory of the United States, its possessions and territories, without a declaration of war or specific statutory authorization shall be considered in accordance with the procedures of section 601(b) of the International Security Assistance and Arms Export Control Act of 1976, except that any such resolution or bill shall be amendable. If such a joint resolution or bill should be vetoed by the President, the time for debate in consideration of the veto message on such measure shall be limited to twenty hours in the Senate and in the House shall be **determined in accordance with the Rules of the House.".**

For text of sec. 601(b) of the International Security Assistance and Arms Export Control Act of 1976, see *Legislation on Foreign Relations Through 2002*, vol. I-A.

[112] Sec. 1(a)(5) of Public Law 104-14 (109 Stat. 186) provided that references to the Committee on Foreign Affairs of the House of Representatives shall be treated as referring to the Committee on International Relations of the House of Representatives.

[113] 50 U.S.C. 1545.

[114] 50 U.S.C. 1546.

[115] 50 U.S.C. 1547.

[116] 50 U.S.C. 1548.

[117] 50 U.S.C. 1541 note.

In: War Powers Resolution after 34 Years...
Editors: Jeremiah E. Sanders

ISBN: 978-1-60692-787-8
© 2010 Nova Science Publishers, Inc.

Chapter 3

WAR POWERS LITIGATION INITIATED BY MEMBERS OF CONGRESS SINCE THE ENACTMENT OF THE WAR POWERS RESOLUTION

M. David Ackerman
Legislative Attorney, American Law Division

SUMMARY

Article I, § 8, of the Constitution confers on Congress the power to "declare War." Modern Presidents, however, have contended that, notwithstanding this clause, they do not need Congressional authorization to use force. Partly in response to that contention, and because of widespread concern that Congress had allowed its war power to atrophy in the Korean and Vietnam conflicts, Congress in 1973 enacted the War Powers Resolution (WPR). The WPR, *inter cilia,* requires the President to report to Congress any time U.S. military forces are introduced into "hostilities or ... situations where imminent involvement in hostilities is clearly indicated by the circumstances." Once such a report is submitted, the WPR requires that the forces must be withdrawn within 60 days (90 days in specified circumstances) unless Congress declares war or otherwise authorizes their continued involvement.

Nonetheless, subsequent Presidents have continued to maintain that they have sufficient authority independent of Congress to initiate the use of military force; and all Presidents from Nixon to Bush have viewed the WPR as trenching on their constitutional powers. Congress has on four occasions enacted authorizations specifically waiving the 60-90 day limitation on the use of force otherwise imposed by the WPR. But in six other instances involving U.S. military involvement in El Salvador, Nicaragua, Grenada, the Persian Gulf conflict between Iraq and Iran, Iraq's invasion of Kuwait (prior to the Congressional authorization), and NATO's action in Kosovo, Presidential avoidance and Congressional inaction have led a number of Members to initiate suits in federal court to compel various Presidents to comply with the reporting and/or troop withdrawal requirements of the Resolution or to otherwise recognize Congress' war powers. A seventh suit, recently decided, sought to enjoin the President from using military force against Iraq on the grounds such an action would exceed the authority conferred by Congress in the statute it adopted in October, 2002.

In every instance to date (with the exception of part of the last decision) the courts have found reasons not to render a decision on the merits of the suits. The courts have variously found the political question doctrine, the equitable/remedial discretion doctrine, the issue of ripeness, and the question of Congressional standing to preclude judicial resolution of the matter. Although not ruling out the possibility that a conflict over the use of force between Congress and the President could require a judicial resolution, the courts so far have deemed the matter to be one for the political branches to resolve.

This report summarizes the seven cases initiated by Members of Congress. It will be updated as circumstances warrant.

INTRODUCTION

Seven times since the enactment of the War Powers Resolution in 1973,[1] Members of Congress have filed suit to force various Presidents to comply with its requirements or otherwise to recognize Congress' war powers under the Constitution. Seven times the federal courts have refused to render a decision on the merits.[2] In four instances the suits have foundered on the political question or equitable discretion doctrines, which the federal courts use to insulate themselves from essentially political disputes. In another case

War Powers Litigation Initiated by Members of Congress since... 139

the suit failed on grounds of standing, and in two cases the suits foundered on the ripeness doctrine.

Article I, § 8, of the Constitution confers on. Congress the power to "declare War"; and Congress has enacted such declarations eleven times in American history. It has also enacted a number of authorizations for the use of military force not rising to the level of a declaration of war.[3] Nonetheless, concern that Congress had allowed its war power to atrophy in the contexts of the Cold War and the wars in Korea and Vietnam led to the enactment in 1973, over President Nixon's veto, of the War Powers Resolution (WPR). The legislation's supporters hoped that its enactment would ensure that a national consensus precedes the use of U.S. armed forces in hostilities abroad. Accordingly, the Resolution requires the President to consult with Congress "in every possible instance" prior to introducing U.S. armed forces into hostilities and to report to Congress within 48 hours when, absent a declaration of war, U.S. armed forces are introduced into "hostilities or .. situations where imminent involvement in hostilities is clearly indicated by the circumstances."[4] Unless Congress authorizes continued involvement by adopting a declaration of war or other authorization, the WPR requires that U.S. troops be withdrawn at the end of 60 days (90 days in certain circumstances).[5]

Presidents from Ford to Bush have submitted more than 100 reports to Congress giving notice of the involvement of U.S. aimed forces in hostile situations.[6] But because all of these Presidents have objected to the War Powers Resolution as unconstitutionally trenching on their constitutional powers, their reports to Congress on the involvement of U.S. troops in hostilities overseas have generally avoided using language that would trigger the time limitation and the consequent need for Congressional authorization for continued involvement.[7] That practice has frustrated numerous lawmakers and has led some to pursue other avenues, including litigation, to compel the President to recognize the legal necessity of obtaining Congressional authorization for the use of force.

Although both the White House and the Members who have initiated the suits have claimed that each will ultimately prevail if the courts ever pass on the merits of the controversy, neither thus far has taken steps that would give the courts a viable statutory or constitutional issue to resolve, rather than a policy dispute. On the one hand, despite periodic Administration claims that it would welcome a court test, the Justice Department has consistently raised threshold obstacles to court challenges such as Member standing to sue and the political question doctrine obstacles which have so far successfully forestalled judicial rulings on the merits. On the other hand, litigation by Members of Congress to force a decision has not been preceded by legislative actions that have been sufficient to create the "irreconcilable conflict" between the executive and legislative branches that might make a judicial decision possible, if not probable.

This report summarizes the seven suits that have been brought by Members of Congress since the enactment of the War Powers Resolution which have alleged Presidential noncompliance with the Resolution and/or the requirements of the Constitution with respect to the involvement of U.S. armed forces in El Salvador, Nicaragua, Grenada, U.S. escort operations in the Persian Gulf, Iraq's invasion of Kuwait, NATO's actions against Yugoslavia, and Iraq's noncompliance with its obligation to disarm.

El Salvador

In *Crockett v. Reagan*[8] in 1982 16 Senators and 13 House Members asked a federal district court to declare that military aid supplied to the government of El Salvador by President Reagan usurped Congress' war powers under the Constitution and violated the War Powers Resolution and the Foreign Assistance Act. In particular, the lawmakers charged that the unreported dispatch of 56 members of the U.S. armed forces as military advisers to war-racked El Salvador constituted a violation of the Resolution. The Reagan Administration moved to dismiss the action on the grounds the suit involved a political question, and the district court granted the motion. The U.S. Court of Appeals for the District of Columbia affirmed.

Examining the categories of political questions set forth in *Baker v. Carr,*[9] the trial court rejected the Administration's arguments that judicial resolution was inappropriate because it would interfere with executive discretion in the foreign affairs field or because the suit involved the apportionment of power between the executive and legislative branches. However, it concluded, judicial resolution was inappropriate because there were no "judicially discoverable and manageable standards for resolution" of the case:

> The questions as to the nature and extent of the United States' **presence** in El Salvador and whether a report under the WPR is mandated because our forces have been subject to hostile fire or are taking part in the war effort are appropriate for congressional, not judicial, investigation. Further, in order to determine the application of the 60-day provision, the Court would be

War Powers Litigation Initiated by Members of Congress since...   141

required to decide at exactly what point in time U.S. forces had been introduced into hostilities or imminent hostilities, and whether that situation continues to exist. This inquiry would be even more inappropriate for the judiciary

The Court lacks the resources and expertise (which are accessible to the Congress) to resolve disputed questions of fact concerning the military situation in El Salvador.[10]

The trial court contrasted the situation in El Salvador with the conflict in Vietnam, noting that the latter conflict had persisted for seven years, resulted in more than a million deaths (including over 50,000 Americans), and involved the expenditure of $100 billion. In El Salvador, the court noted, the American military personnel were relatively few in number and had suffered no casualties. Accordingly, the court concluded, the question of whether U.S. forces had been introduced into hostilities in El Salvador was less obvious than Vietnam, and "[t]he subtleties of fact-finding in this situation should be left to the political branches."[11]

The court declined to speculate about the kind of Congressional actions that might give rise to a judicially manageable issue, noting simply that "Congress has taken absolutely no action that could be interpreted to have that effect." However, it did state that "were Congress to pass a resolution to the effect that a report was required under the WPR, or to the effect that the forces should be withdrawn, and the President disregarded it, a constitutional impasse appropriate for judicial resolution would be presented."[12]

On appeal the United States Court of Appeals for the District of Columbia affirmed the dismissal in a brief per *curiam* opinion "for the reasons stated by the District Court."

Nicaragua

In *Sanchez-Espinoza v. Reagan*[13] in 1983, twelve Members of the House of Representatives, 12 Nicaraguan citizens, and 2 United States citizens sued for damages, injunctive relief and a declaration that President Reagan and other executive officials had violated various federal statutes, including the War Powers Resolution, by supporting paramilitary operations designed to overthrow the government of Nicaragua. A federal district court dismissed the litigation as raising nonjusticiable political questions, and the U.S. Court of Appeals for the District of Columbia again affirmed.

The district court stated as a predicate that the separation of powers doctrine affords the judiciary a very limited role in matters related to foreign policy and national security, stating that such matters are largely, if not exclusively, entrusted to the political branches. The court then examined various benchmarks established by the Supreme Court for application of the political question doctrine, and found three of the criteria established in *Baker v. Carr, supra,* for determining whether a question falls into that category to be particularly relevant.

In accord with the *Crockett* decision, the district court held that resolution of the issue raised by the Congressional plaintiffs called for fact-finding that exceeded its competence. In political question terms the court said that resolution of the issue raised by the lawmakers was difficult if not impossible because of the lack of "judicially discoverable and manageable standards."[14] According to the court, the circumstances before it were even more egregious than those in *Crockett* since "the covert activities of CIA operatives in Nicaragua and Honduras are perforce even less judicially discoverable than the level of participation by U.S. military personnel in hostilities in El Salvador."[15] In addition, the court stated, in light of the wide differences between the President and Congress concerning Nicaraguan policy, "[a] second reason for finding this matter non-justiciable is the impossibility of our undertaking independent resolution without expressing a lack of the respect due coordinate branches of government."[16]

Finally, the court averred, because Administration policy was under constant review at both ends of Pennsylvania Avenue, attempts at a resolution by the judiciary presented a real danger of embarrassment from multifarious pronouncements by various departments on the question of U.S. involvement. "Such an occurrence," it said, "would, undoubtedly, rattle the delicate diplomatic balance that is required in the foreign affairs arena."[17]

The United States Court of Appeals for the District of Columbia affirmed on appeal. With respect to the claim of the Congressional plaintiffs that the assistance given the *contras* by the executive branch violated the Boland amendment forbidding the CIA and the Department of Defense from providing any such assistance, the court noted that the Boland amendment was an appropriations rider and had expired at the end of fiscal 1983. As a consequence, it held that the claim had to be dismissed as moot. With respect to the Congressional plaintiffs' claim that the assistance to the *contras* amounted to waging war and that, as a consequence, they had "been deprived of their [constitutional] right to participate in the decision to declare war," the appellate court, citing *Crockett,* held that the "war powers issue presented a nonjusticiable political question.[18] Justice Ginsburg filed an opinion concurring in the latter ruling on the grounds the issue was "not ripe for judicial review." She stressed that the political branches had not as yet reached "a constitutional impasse" on the issue. Congress, she said, has "formidable weapons at its disposal ... [b]ut no gauntlet has been thrown down here by a majority of the Members of Congress."

Grenada

In *Conyers v. Reagan*[19] in 1984, eleven Members of the House challenged the President Reagan's use of force in Grenada as an executive usurpation of Congress' war powers under the Constitution. The federal district court dismissed the action on the basis of the doctrine of equitable/remedial discretion, which counsels the courts to refrain from hearing cases brought by Congressional plaintiffs who can obtain substantial relief by legislative action. In particular, the court said, "[w]hat is available to these plaintiffs are the institutional remedies afforded to Congress as a body; specifically, the War Powers Resolution ...."[20]

On appeal the United States Court of Appeals for the District of Columbia affirmed largely on mootness grounds because the invasion had been concluded. Congressional plaintiffs' attempt on appeal to raise the war powers issue because of the post-invasion presence of U.S. military personnel in Grenada, the appellate court said, came too late and did not alter the moot character of the case.

PERSIAN GULF CONFLICT BETWEEN IRAN AND IRAQ

In *Lowry v. Reagan*[21] in 1987, a federal district court dismissed an action brought by 110 Members of the House to compel President Reagan to file a report under the War Powers Resolution in connection with the initiation of U.S. escort operations of reflagged Kuwaiti oil tankers in the Persian Gulf during the war between Iran and Iraq. The grounds for dismissal this time were both the equitable discretion and political question doctrines. Once again, the U.S. Court of Appeals for the District of Columbia affirmed.

144 M. David Ackerman

Taking note of the divisions in Congress with respect to the applicability of the War Powers Resolution and the wisdom of the escort operation, the district court observed:

> Although styled as a dispute between the legislative and executive branches of government, this lawsuit evidences and indeed is a by-product of political disputes within Congress regarding the applicability of the War Powers Resolution to the Persian Gulf situation.[22]

The court also took note of several unsuccessful legislative efforts to force Presidential compliance with the law and to revise and strengthen the War Powers Resolution and concluded that the plaintiffs' "dispute is 'primarily with [their] fellow legislators.'"[23] Accordingly, the court said it was proper as a matter of equitable discretion to withhold the exercise of jurisdiction and the requested relief. It noted, however, that if Congress enacted legislation to enforce the Resolution and the President ignored it, "a question ripe for judicial review" would be presented.

Analyzing the complex international political situation as it impacted on the Gulf in light of the benchmarks set in. *Baker v. Carr, supra,* the court also concluded "that plaintiffs' request for declaratory relief presents a nonjusticiable political question.[24] A judicial resolution of the matter, it said, would risk "the potentiality of embarrassment ... from multifarious pronouncements by various departments on one question.[25]

In an unpublished opinion the United States Court of Appeals for the District of Columbia dismissed the appeal on grounds the suit presented a nonjusticiable political question and on grounds of mootness.[26] By the time of its decision Iran and Iraq had agreed to a cease-fire.

Iraq's Invasion of Kuwait

In *Dellums v. Bush*[27] in 1990, fifty-three House Members and one Senator sought to enjoin President Bush from initiating an offensive attack against Iraq without first obtaining Congressional authorization. Iraq had invaded and occupied Kuwait in August, 1990; and President Bush, with the sanction of the United Nations Security Council, had assembled a massive military force in the vicinity with the apparent purpose of reversing that occupation. He had not, however, sought or obtained Congressional authorization for the use of

War Powers Litigation Initiated by Members of Congress since... 145

force. In those circumstances a federal district court ruled that the issue was not yet ripe for judicial decision and dismissed the case.

In contrast to the preceding decisions, the court concluded that neither the political question nor the equitable/remedial discretion doctrines precluded it from resolving the question presented by the suit. It said that "in principle, an injunction may issue at the request of Members of Congress to prevent the conduct of a war which is about to be carried on without congressional authorization."[28] On the political question issue, it noted the "clear" language of the Constitution authorizing Congress to declare war and the absence of any serious factual dispute that the initiation of combat operations against Iraq by several hundred thousand troops would constitute a war. It further asserted that the courts were not excluded from resolving suits merely because they involved questions of foreign policy. On the remedial discretion issue, the court concluded, without further explanation, that the plaintiffs "cannot gain substantial relief by persuasion of their colleagues alone.[29]

Nonetheless, the court refused to resolve the case on the merits on the grounds that not all the elements necessary for a decision were yet present, *i.e.*, the case was not yet "ripe" for decision. On the one hand, it noted, a majority of the Congress had taken no action on the matter of whether Congressional authorization was needed in this instance; the plaintiffs, it observed, represented only about 10 percent of the Congress. On the other hand, it said, it was also not yet irrevocably certain that the President intended to initiate a war against Iraq. Both elements, it asserted, were necessary before a court could address the constitutional issue. It said that a majority of Congress had to request relief "from an infringement on its constitutional war- declaration power," and the Executive Branch had to be shown to be committed to "a definitive course of action."

No appeal was taken from this decision.

NATO's Air War in Kosovo and Yugoslavia

In *Campbell v. Clinton*[30] in 1999, twenty-six Members of the House initiated a suit asking for a declaratory judgment that U.S. participation in NATO's military actions against Yugoslavia in the Kosovo situation violated Congress' constitutional power to declare war or otherwise authorize military action and that the War Powers Resolution required the termination of U. S. participation "no later than sixty calendar days after March 24, 1999" (the date NATO began bombing Yugoslavia) unless Congress authorized continued

U.S. involvement. A federal district court dismissed the action on the grounds the Members lacked standing to bring the suit, and the U.S. Court of Appeals for the District of Columbia affirmed on the same grounds. The Supreme Court denied a request to review the decision.

The district court noted that the House and Senate had taken a number of actions with respect to NATO's offensive in Yugoslavia. On March 23, 1999, the Senate had approved a concurrent resolution authorizing the President to "conduct military air operations and missile strikes in cooperation with our NATO allies against ... Yugoslavia" by a vote of 58-41. On March 24, the day the attacks began, the court said, the House approved a resolution stating that it "supports the members of the United States Armed Forces who are engaged in military operations against the Federal Republic of Yugoslavia and recognizes their professionalism, dedication, patriotism, and courage" by a vote of 424-1. On April 28 the House defeated a joint resolution declaring war on Yugoslavia by a vote of 2-427; rejected the concurrent resolution that had been approved by the Senate on a tie vote of 213-213; rejected a concurrent resolution directing the President to withdraw U.S. armed forces from their involvement in the NATO campaign by a vote of 139-290; and passed a bill barring the use of Department of Defense funds for the deployment of ground forces in Yugoslavia without specific authorization by voice vote. Finally, the court noted that Congress had enacted a supplemental emergency appropriations bill on May 20 providing funds for the conflict in Yugoslavia but had not stated, *as* required to satisfy the War Powers Resolution, that the measure constituted specific statutory authorization for the continued involvement of U.S. armed forces.

The trial court stated that the lawsuit raised "especially grave separation of powers issues" and observed that courts traditionally have been reluctant "to intercede in disputes between the political branches of government that involve matters of war and peace."[31] It rejected the argument, however, that courts can never adjudicate disputes that involve foreign relations. But it said that in this instance it did not need to determine whether the case was properly subject to judicial decision because the Congressional plaintiffs lacked standing to bring the suit. While the D.C. Circuit had in the past followed a fairly relaxed standard with respect to Congressional standing, it said, the Supreme Court in *Raines v. Byrd*[32] had "dramatically" altered the legal landscape. In that case, it asserted, the Court had held that members of Congress who voted against the Line Item Veto Act[33] lacked standing to challenge the constitutionality of the Act because they retained a political remedy, namely, the repeal of the Act or the exemption of individual

War Powers Litigation Initiated by Members of Congress since... 147

appropriations from its purview. Any injury they suffered with respect to their votes on future appropriations bills and to the balance of power between Congress and the President, the Court had ruled, was "wholly abstract and widely dispersed" and lacked the particularity and concreteness necessary to confer standing.

Thus, the court said, it was not sufficient in this case for the Congressional plaintiffs to allege simply that the President had ignored the declaration of war clause of the Constitution or the War Powers Resolution. Nor, it held, was it sufficient to allege that Congress had taken actions in this instance which the President had nullified or ignored by initiating and continuing U.S. involvement in the NATO campaign. For Members of Congress to have standing, the court said, there had to be a genuine "constitutional impasse." Had Congress directed the President to withdraw U.S. forces and he had refused to do so, or had Congress refused to appropriate funds for the air strikes and the President had used other funds for that purpose, the court suggested, "that likely would have constituted an actual confrontation sufficient to confer standing on legislative plaintiffs."[34] But the Congressional votes here, the court stated, did "not provide the President with such an unambiguous directive" but instead sent "distinctly mixed messages." The court concluded:

> Where, as here, Congress has taken actions that send conflicting signals with respect to the effect and significance of the allegedly nullified votes, there is no actual confrontation or impasse between the executive and legislative branches and thus no legislative standing.[35]

The court also noted that the 26 plaintiffs in this case had not been authorized by the House to institute the suit.

On February 18, 2000, the U.S. Court of Appeals for the District of Columbia affirmed on standing grounds. The court noted that in *Coleman v. Miller*[36] the Supreme Court had ruled that state legislators who claimed their votes had been sufficient to defeat the ratification of a constitutional amendment had standing to challenge the actions of the Kansas Secretary of State in authenticating the amendment as approved, because the effect of the authentication was to nullify the effectiveness of their votes. In *Campbell* the appellate court interpreted *Coleman* to mean that the legislators had standing only if they had no legislative remedy whatsoever. But in this case, it concluded, "appellants ... continued ... to enjoy ample legislative power to have stopped prosecution of the 'war'":

> Congress certainly could have passed a law forbidding the use of U.S. forces in the Yugoslav campaign .... Congress always retains appropriations authority and could have cut off funds for the American role in the conflict .... And there always remains the possibility of impeachment should a President act in disregard of Congress' authority on these matters.

This reasoning, the court said, applied to the plaintiffs' claims regarding both the War Powers Resolution and the constitutional allocation of the war power.

Each of the three judges on the appellate panel filed concurring opinions as well. Judge Silberman stated that in his opinion the plaintiffs' claims (and, apparently, any other war power claim) should also be dismissed on grounds of nonjusticiability, because "[w]e lack 'judicially discoverable and manageable standards' for addressing them, and the War Powers Clause claim implicates the political question doctrine." The 60-day withdrawal mandate of the War Powers Resolution, he stated, is triggered only if U.S. forces are engaged in hostilities or are in imminent danger of hostilities. But that standard, he contended, "is not precise enough and too obviously calls for a political judgment to be one suitable for judicial determinations." Similarly, he asserted, there is no constitutional test for determining what constitutes a war or when a declaration of war is necessary, and the judiciary is ill-equipped to engage in the fact-finding involved in making such determinations. Finally, Judge Silberman said, such issues are necessarily ones of "the greatest sensitivity for our foreign relations" on which conflicting pronouncements by the different branches of government ought to be avoided.

Judge Tatel's concurring opinion took issue with this assertion that the case presented a nonjusticiable political question. Determining whether war exists or not, he contended, "is no more standardless than any other question regarding the constitutionality of government action"; and, he said, courts have frequently made that determination. Moreover, he asserted, the plaintiffs' claim regarding the War Powers Resolution did not even require the court to make that determination but only whether U.S. armed forces were introduced into "hostilities." "One of the most important functions of Article III courts," he said, "[is] determining the proper constitutional allocation of power among the branches of government." Claims that a case involves issues of foreign relations and risks the danger of government speaking with "multifarious voices," Judge Tatel concluded, should not prevent a court from determining "whether the President exceeded his constitutional or statutory authority by conducting the air campaign in Yugoslavia":

> If in 1799 the Supreme Court could recognize that sporadic battles between American and French vessels amounted to a state of war, and if in 1862 it could examine the record of hostilities and conclude that a state of war existed with the confederacy, then surely we, looking at similar evidence, could determine whether months of daily airstrikes involving 800 U.S. aircraft flying more than 20,000 sorties and causing thousands of enemy casualties amounted to "war" within the meaning of Article I, section 8, clause 11.

Finally, Judge Randolph contended that the court had misapplied the Supreme Court's decisions in *Coleman* and *Raines* but that the case still should have been dismissed on the grounds of standing and also of mootness. The plaintiffs lacked standing, he said, not because they retained legislative remedies for what they claimed to be the President's illegal actions but because their votes had not, as required by *Raines,* been completely nullified. In fact, he said, their vote against a declaration of war deprived the President of the greatly expanded powers he obtains under a number of statutes in a declared war and deprived him as well of the "authority to introduce ground troops into the conflict." Thus, he asserted, "plaintiffs' votes against declaring war were not for naught," and for that reason they lacked standing to sue. The reasoning of the majority opinion was wrong, he contended, because it "confused the right to vote in the future with the nullification of a vote in the past." In addition, he said, the case was moot, because hostilities had ended at least by June 21, 1999. If the issue were one "capable of repetition, yet evading review," Judge Randolph noted, it would not be moot. But neither element was satisfied here. The D.C. Circuit's prior decision in *Conyers v. Reagan, supra,* he stated, had held that wars initiated without congressional approval are not matters that inherently evade review. Moreover, he said, it was doubtful that the statutory claim that the President continued the war for more than 60 days without congressional authorization met the "capable of repetition" element. President Clinton, he noted, was the first President "who arguably violated the 60-day provision," and the plaintiffs themselves stated that in modern times most U.S. attacks on foreign nations "will be over quickly, by which they mean less than 60 days."

The Congressional appellants sought further review in the Supreme Court; but on October 2, 2000, the Court denied review.

Regime Change and Disarmament in Iraq

In *Doe v. Bush*[37] twelve Members of the House of Representatives, three members of the military, and fifteen parents of service members instituted suit to enjoin President Bush from launching a military invasion of Iraq to remove Saddam Hussein from power and to enforce Iraq's disarmament. Notwithstanding enactment in October, 2002, of the "Authorization for the Use of Force Against Iraq Resolution,[38] the plaintiffs contended that the authorization unconstitutionally delegated to the President Congress' power to declare war or, alternatively, that an invasion of Iraq would exceed the authority granted by the authorization. On February 24, 2003, a federal district court held the suit to raise a nonjusticiable political question and dismissed the case. On March 13, 2003, the U.S. Court of Appeals for the First Circuit affirmed on the basis that the issues in the case were not ripe for judicial review and that the October authorization did not constitute an unlawful delegation of Congress' constitutional authority.

Citing *Baker v. Carr, supra,* the trial court held that judicial resolution of a war powers issue would be appropriate "only when the actions taken by Congress and those taken by the Executive manifest clear, resolute conflict." The Constitution, it said, commits the conduct of the nation's foreign relations to the political branches of the federal government. As a consequence, it stated, "absent a clear abdication of this constitutional responsibility by the political branches, the judiciary has no role to play." In this instance, the court ruled, there was no "intractable constitutional gridlock." In the October, 2002, authorization, it noted, "Congress has expressly endorsed the President's use of the military against Iraq"; and as of the day of its decision, it said, "the President, for his part, has not irrevocably committed our armed forces to military conflict in Iraq." Given the "day to day fluidity" in the situation, the court concluded, the case raised "political questions ... which are beyond the authority of a federal court to resolve."

On March 13, 2003, the U.S. Court of Appeals affiiiiied. Eschewing reliance on the political question doctrine, the appellate court held that there was no "constitutional impasse" between Congress and the President regarding the use of force against Iraq and, as a consequence, the issue was not ripe for judicial review. Ripeness, the court said, "mixes various mutually reinforcing constitutional and prudential considerations." One, it stated, is to prevent rulings on "abstract disagreements." A second is "to avoid unnecessary constitutional decisions." A third element simply recognizes that courts can benefit "from a focus sharpened by particular facts." In this instance, it asserted, "[m]any important questions remain unanswered about whether there will be a war, and, if so, under what conditions." Even if the plaintiffs' assertion that the October authorization does not authorize the use of force against Iraq is granted, it said, "it is impossible to say yet whether or not those commands will be obeyed." "If courts may ever decide whether military action contravenes congressional authority," the court concluded, "they surely cannot do so unless and until the available facts make it possible to define the issues with clarity."

The court did, however, reach the merits of the issue on the plaintiffs' other claim, namely, that the discretionary authority to use force conferred on the President by the October authorization unconstitutionally delegated Congress' power to declare war. That issue might be "clearly framed," the appellate court stated, "if Congress gave absolute discretion to the President to start a war at his or her will." But, it said, "the mere fact that the October Resolution grants some discretion to the President fails to raise a sufficiently clear constitutional issue." Even with respect to the exercise of powers that are entirely legislative in nature, it noted, the Supreme Court has upheld "enactments which leave discretion to the executive branch ... as long as they offer some 'intelligible principle' to guide that discretion." Moreover, it stressed, in the area of foreign affairs the Court has made clear that "the nondelegation doctrine has even less applicability ...." In addition, it said, "there is [no] clear evidence of congressional abandonment of the authority to declare war to the President." For more than a decade, it noted, Congress "has been deeply involved in significant debate, activity, and authorization connected to our relations with Iraq ...." The October resolution itself, the court said, "spells out justifications for a war and frames itself as an 'authorization' of such a war." These circumstances, the court concluded, "do not warrant judicial intervention."

On March 18, 2003, the appellate court rejected an emergency petition for rehearing of its decision. The court stated:

> Although some of the contingencies described in our opinion appear to have been resolved, others have not. Most importantly, Congress has taken no action which presents a "fully developed dispute between the two elected branches." Thus, the case continues not to be fit for judicial review.

CONCLUSION

Historically, the courts have been reluctant to act in cases involving issues of national security and foreign policy. The enactment of the War Powers Resolution in 1973 does not appear to have altered that situation. Seven efforts by lawmakers since enactment of the Resolution effectively calling upon federal judges to put traditional scruples aside have proven to be unavailing. In each and every case brought to resolve the Presidential-Congressional impasse over the law and/or the constitutional division of the war power since the WPR's enactment, the courts have concluded that the factors calling for abstention outweigh those in favor of involvement. The courts have variously relied on the political question doctrine, the equitable/remedial discretion doctrine, ripeness, mootness, and Congressional standing. In the one ruling arguably on the merits, the U.S. Court of Appeals for the First Circuit ruled that a discretionary grant of authority to the President to use force under specified circumstances does not constitute an unlawful delegation of Congress' power to declare war.

The courts have made clear, however, that while formidable, none of the aforementioned procedural barriers constitutes an insurmountable obstacle to resolving the statutory or constitutional issues concerning war powers. All of the opinions to date indicate that the barrier to the exercise of jurisdiction stems from the posture of the cases, not some institutional shortcoming. If the courts are to be believed, both statutory and constitutional war powers issues can be judicially determined if a legal, as distinguished from a political, impasse is created. It has been suggested that this can come about by Congressional action that directs the President to take a particular action, or bars him from doing so, and by Presidential noncompliance. Absent such an irreconcilable conflict, however, it seems unlikely that the courts will venture into this politically and constitutionally charged thicket.

End Notes

[1] P.L. 93-148 (Nov. 7, 1973); 87 Stat. 555; 50 U.S.C. §§ 1541 *at seq.* (1994).

[2] *But see infra* Doe v. Bush, 2003 U.S. App. LEXIS 4477 (1" Cir. 2003) (rejecting on the merits a contention that Congress in the "Authorization for the Use of Force Against Iraq Resolution of 2002" unconstitutionally delegated its war-declaring power to the President).

[3] For a thorough review of Congress' actions in enacting declarations of war and otherwise authorizing the use of force and of the legal consequences of these actions, *see* CRS Report

War Powers Litigation Initiated by Members of Congress since... 153

RL31133, *Declarations of War and Authorizations for the Use of Force: Historical Background and Legal Implications.*

[4] 50 U.S.C. § 1543.

[5] *Id. § 1544.*

[6] *See* CRS Issue Brief IB81050, War Powers Resolution: Presidential Compliance.

[7] The one exception to that practice was President Ford's report to Congress on the U.S. response to the seizure of the *Mayaguez* in 1975 by Cambodian naval vessels, which specifically cited the section of the Resolution (§ 4(a)(1)) triggering the time limit. For a detailed description and analysis of Presidential compliance with the War Powers Resolution, see CRS Report RL31185, *The War Powers Resolution: After Twenty-Eight Years.*

[8] Crockett v. Reagan, 558 F. Supp. 893 (D.D.C. 1982), *gird per curiam,* 720 F.2d 1355, 1357 (D.C.Cir. 1983), *cert. den.,* 467 U.S. 1251 (1984).

[9] 369 U.S. 186 (1962). The Supreme Court in *Baker* identified the possible dimensions of the political question doctrine as follows:

It is apparent that several formulations which vary slightly according to the settings in which the questions arise may describe a political question, although each has one or more elements which identify it as essentially a function of the separation of powers. Prominent on the surface of any case held to involve a political question is found a textually demonstrable constitutional commitment of the issue to a coordinate political department; or a lack of judicially discoverable and manageable standards for resolving it; or the impossibility of deciding without an initial policy determination of a kind clearly for nonjudicial discretion; or the impossibility of a court's undertaking independent resolution without expressing lack of respect due coordinate branches of government; or an unusual need for unquestioning adherence to a political decision already made; or the potentiality of embarrassment from multifarious pronouncements by various departments on one question. *Id.* at 217.

[10] 558 F.Supp. at 898.

[11] *Id.* at 899.

[12] *Id.* at 899.

[13] Sanchez-Espinoza v. Reagan, 568 F. Supp. 596 (D.D.C. 1983), *aff'd,* 770 F.2d 202 (D.C. Cir. 1985).

[14] 568 F. Supp. at 600.

[15] *Id.*

[16] *Id.*

[17] *Id.* The court noted in a footnote that another reason for dismissing the suit lay in the doctrine of equitable or remedial discretion. As explained by the court, that doctrine counsels judicial restraint where the Congressional plaintiffs could obtain substantial relief through Congressional action and the suit represents, as a consequence, a "circumvent(ion of) the process of democratic decisionmaking." *See* 568 F. Supp. 600-601, n. 5.

[18] 770 F.2d at 210.

[19] Conyers v. Reagan, 578 F. Supp. 324 (D.D.C. 1984), *aff'd,* 765 F.2d 1124 (D.C. Cir. 1985).

[20] 578 F. Supp. at 327.

[21] Lowry v. Reagan, 676 F. Supp. 333 (D.D.C. 1987), *aff'd,* No. 87-5426 (D.C. Cir. 1988).

[22] *Id.* at 338.

[23] *Id.* at 339.

[24] *Id.* at 340.

[25] *Id.* at 340, quoting Baker v. Carr, *supra,* at 217.

[26] Lowry v. Reagan, No. 87-5426 (D.C. Cir. 1988).

[27] 752 F.Supp, 1141 (D.D.C. 1990).

[28] *Id.* at 1149.

[29] *Id.* at 1149.

[30] Campbell v. Clinton, 52 F.Supp.2d 34 (D.D.C. 1999), *aff'd,* 203 F.2d 19 (D.C. Cir.), *cert. den.,* 531 U.S. 815 (2000).

154 M. David Ackerman

[31] *Id.* at 40.

[32] 521 U.S. 811 (1997).

[33] 2 U.S.C. § 691.

[34] 521 U.S. at 43.

[35] *Id.* at 44.

[36] 307 U.S. 433 (1939).

[37] Doe v. Bush, 2003 U.S. Dist. LEXIS 2773 (D. Mass. Feb. 27, 2003), *aff'd,* 2003 U.S. App. LEXIS 447 (1" Cir. Mar. 13, 2003), *petition for rehearing denied,* 2003 U.S. App. LEXIS 4830 (1' Cir. Mar. 18, 2003).

[38] P.L. 107-243 (Oct. 16, 2002). In its operative section the statute authorizes the President to use the armed forces of the United States "as he determines to be necessary and appropriate in order to — (1) defend the national security of the United States against the continuing threat posed by Iraq; and (2) enforce all relevant United Nations Security Council resolutions regarding Iraq."

CHAPTER SOURCES

The following chapters have been previously published:

Chapter 1 – This is an edited, excerpted and augmented edition of a United States Congressional Research Service publication, Report Order Code RL33532, dated June 11, 2008.

Chapter 2 – This is an edited, excerpted and augmented edition of a United States Congressional Research Service publication, Report Order Code RL32267, dated March 10, 2008.

Chapter 3 – This is an edited, excerpted and augmented edition of a United States Congressional Research Service publication, Report Order Code RL30352, dated March 19, 2003.

INDEX

A

administration, 49, 108
administrative, 108, 109
aggression, x, 2, 12, 41, 48, 54, 55, 83
aid, 10, 13, 16, 32, 37, 42, 57, 59, 63, 77, 91, 116, 133, 135, 140
air, 7, 8, 11, 13, 54, 55, 61, 62, 66, 67, 72, 76, 91, 94, 95, 97, 100, 106, 132, 146, 147, 148
Air Force, 48
air traffic, 13, 76
airports, 48
allies, 7, 8, 65, 72, 73, 81, 106, 112, 146
amendments, 29, 62, 73, 83, 86, 88, 131, 134
analysts, 38
anti-terrorism, xi, 28, 117
appendix, 90
application, ix, x, xi, 1, 22, 27, 36, 48, 130, 140, 142
appropriations, x, 2, 8, 35, 37, 38, 73, 76, 86, 89, 142, 146, 147, 148
appropriations bills, 147
Appropriations Committee, 5, 46
argument, 146
armed conflict, 31
assassination, 45
assignment, 35, 36, 129
atrophy, xii, 137, 139

attacks, x, 2, 3, 11, 24, 26, 29, 61, 62, 66, 79, 80, 81, 84, 86, 94, 95, 97, 102, 112, 146, 149
authentication, 147
avoidance, xii, 138
AWACS, 93, 123
awareness, 23, 85

B

back, 34, 127, 128
barrier, 152
barriers, 152
benchmarks, 142, 144
binding, 16, 39, 63, 70, 72, 76
biological weapons, 10, 59
bipartisan, 55
boats, 13, 49, 76, 91, 95
Bosnia-Herzegovina, 19, 20, 67, 68, 69, 70, 71, 100, 101, 120, 121
burning, 11

C

carrier, 49
cast, 38
cease-fire, 10, 37, 51, 59, 60, 65, 74, 144
censorship, 58
certification, 87
certifications, 13, 75
channels, 62

Index

CIA, 142

cilia, xii, 137

citizens, 13, 17, 19, 20, 23, 37, 40, 47, 51, 73, 75, 76, 80, 81, 86, 91, 92, 93, 95, 96, 99, 102, 103, 104, 105, 106, 109, 112, 115, 116, 118, 120, 131, 141

civil war, 49

civilian, 10, 58, 65, 95

cloture, 83

coastal communities, 91

Cold War, ix, xi, 27, 40, 52, 90, 139

Committee on Armed Services, 132

communication, 29, 85

communities, 91

competence, 142

complement, 32, 107

compliance, x, xi, 1, 2, 11, 13, 25, 28, 40, 43, 57, 59, 65, 75, 84, 89, 97, 134, 144, 153

concreteness, 147

confidence, 70

conflict, x, xi, xii, 2, 11, 28, 29, 32, 64, 66, 70, 85, 86, 138, 140, 141, 146, 148, 149, 150, 152

conformity, 38

confrontation, 31, 147

congress, 7

Congressional Record, 131, 133, 134

consensus, 7, 24, 65, 71, 74, 139

Constitution, xii, 3, 4, 6, 7, 9, 13, 24, 28, 30, 36, 37, 38, 39, 42, 52, 56, 60, 64, 72, 74, 77, 80, 124, 132, 137, 138, 139, 140, 143, 145, 147, 150

constraints, 53

construction, 75, 86

consulting, 51, 86, 132

control, 5, 10, 11, 16, 44, 51, 53, 59, 60, 61, 62, 63, 74, 79, 85, 102, 107

counter-terror, 18, 19, 20, 116, 119, 120, 121

counterterrorism, 19, 114

Court of Appeals, 9, 74, 140, 141, 142, 143, 144, 146, 147, 150, 152

courts, xii, 4, 28, 40, 47, 51, 89, 138, 139, 143, 145, 146, 148, 150, 152

covert action, 135

crimes, 108

criticism, 55, 68

CRS, 4, 6, 7, 9, 12, 15, 17, 26, 130, 132, 133, 134, 152, 153

cyclone, 135

D

danger, 32, 49, 76, 131, 142, 148

death, 79

deaths, 16, 62, 141

debt, 47

decision making, 41

decisions, x, xi, 1, 2, 28, 29, 55, 59, 65, 66, 89, 145, 149, 150

defense, 8, 11, 18, 19, 20, 42, 71, 73, 75, 78, 95, 119, 120, 121, 131

Defense Authorization Act, 44, 53, 62, 67, 74, 132

definition, 31

delivery, 6, 64, 111, 112, 113

democracy, 79, 99

Department of Defense, 68, 132, 142, 146

Department of State, 5, 42, 91, 132, 135

Desert Storm, 10, 11, 55, 58, 133

destruction, 10, 59, 94

detachment, 111, 112, 113

disaster, 105, 110, 135

disaster assistance, 105

disaster relief, 135

discretionary, 151, 152

dismantlement, 78

disputes, 138, 144, 146

distress, 95

division, ix, 1, 152

domestic conflict, 104

draft, 79, 82, 83

drug trafficking, 51

duration, 14, 33, 77, 81, 103, 112, 116, 125

duties, 45

Index

E

electronic surveillance, 93
embargo, 13, 54, 66, 67, 75, 76, 98, 100
Emergency Assistance, 45
emergency relief, 58
employees, 102, 103, 104
engagement, 79
environment, 61, 110, 111, 113
erosion, 3
evacuation, 91, 93, 99, 102, 103, 104, 105, 109, 115, 116, 122, 123, 131, 134
evening, 79
exclusion, 66, 99
execution, 30, 124
Executive Branch, 145
exercise, x, 2, 6, 26, 48, 64, 84, 89, 144, 151, 152
expertise, 141

F

fear, 86
federal courts, 138
Federal District Court, 7, 8, 24, 72, 73
federal government, 150
Federal Trade Commission, 130
fighters, 3, 21, 114, 116, 121, 122, 123
finance, 38
financial support, 88
financing, 115, 117
fire, 10, 14, 37, 44, 51, 59, 60, 65, 74, 78, 94, 95, 103, 140, 144
flexibility, 5, 22, 29, 31, 85, 86
flight, 103
flow, 16, 63
foreign affairs, 140, 142, 151
foreign nation, 4, 32, 37, 40, 81, 112, 125, 149
foreign person, 102
foreign policy, 23, 29, 85, 89, 142, 145, 152
Foreign Relations Committee, 34, 35, 41, 43, 51, 54, 63, 68, 134
fraud, 51

freedom, 40, 48, 79, 94
fulfillment, x, 2, 125
funding, 8, 9, 54, 73, 74, 78, 134
funds, 5, 6, 8, 13, 16, 24, 44, 46, 53, 55, 60, 63, 66, 67, 68, 69, 70, 72, 73, 75, 76, 86, 87, 146, 147, 148

G

gangs, 61
goals, 11, 16, 56, 60, 62, 84, 116
government, vi, 7, 10, 14, 17, 42, 44, 51, 54, 58, 70, 72, 77, 93, 95, 103, 104, 105, 106, 108, 111, 112, 113, 123, 129, 140, 141, 142, 144, 146, 148, 150, 153
GPO, 130, 134
grants, 28, 151
groups, 10, 44, 58, 59
guidelines, 41
Gulf War, 11, 40, 54, 58, 82

H

harm, 49
hearing, 24, 143
heart, 37, 39, 114
heat, 122
helicopters, 19, 20, 44, 91, 92, 94, 95, 107, 120
high-level, 35, 129
hips, 62
House Appropriations Committee, 46
humanitarian, 6, 10, 15, 53, 58, 61, 62, 64, 91, 97, 103, 106, 108, 109, 111, 112, 113, 117, 135
humanitarian aid, 135

I

Immigration and Nationality Act, 38
impeachment, 148
implementation, 11, 26, 46, 50, 57, 60, 66, 67, 68, 69, 70, 84
in situ, x, 1, 32, 49

160 Index

independence, 10, 59
indication, 31
industrial, 123
infrastructure, 69, 101
infringement, 4, 36, 145
initiation, 143, 145
injunction, 56, 145
INS, 38
inspection, 12, 59
inspectors, 59
instability, 17, 118
integrity, 51
intelligence, 89, 123, 131
intentions, 59
interaction, 89
international law, 4
international terrorism, 25, 48, 80
intervention, xi, 28, 74, 151

J

joining, 14, 77
judge, 9, 47, 74, 108
judges, 56, 148, 152
judgment, 30, 41, 89, 124, 145, 148
judiciary, 141, 142, 148, 150
jurisdiction, 16, 55, 62, 89, 144, 152
justice, 95
Justice Department, 139
justification, 42

K

killing, 49

L

land, 10, 44, 45, 54, 55
language, 8, 15, 25, 35, 68, 73, 74, 78, 79,
   81, 86, 139, 145
law, xi, xii, 4, 8, 12, 24, 25, 27, 28, 30, 33,
   35, 38, 39, 48, 51, 56, 57, 60, 67, 68, 69,
   72, 73, 80, 83, 93, 108, 111, 112, 113,
   126, 129, 144, 148, 152

lawsuits, 89
leadership, 13, 22, 23, 31, 48, 55, 71, 76, 79,
   80, 88, 89, 91, 114
leaks, 93
legislation, x, 2, 6, 23, 25, 30, 36, 43, 45,
   46, 47, 50, 53, 54, 55, 64, 80, 82, 83, 89,
   90, 91, 128, 129, 134, 139, 144
legislative proposals, 43
limitation, xii, 29, 47, 85, 89, 91, 135, 138,
   139
litigation, 74, 139, 140, 141
location, 10
logistics, 62, 71, 104, 107, 108, 109

M

maritime, 114, 115, 116, 117
marsh, 10
measures, 6, 8, 11, 13, 32, 42, 48, 50, 51,
   53, 54, 55, 61, 62, 64, 65, 70, 71, 72, 76,
   87, 92
membership, 126
men, 32, 70
messages, 147
military aid, 140
mines, 94
minority, 11, 23, 60, 88, 89
missiles, 10, 48, 49, 60, 94, 98, 106
missions, 5, 15, 53, 66, 78, 98
morning, 79
motion, 42, 79, 140
movement, 115, 116, 117, 129
multilateral, 51, 54
mutiny, 104

N

nation, 4, 14, 32, 33, 37, 40, 77, 125, 150
National Defense Authorization Act, 74
national emergency, 3, 30, 37, 124
national security, 13, 25, 26, 75, 84, 142,
   152, 154
National Security Council, 23
negotiating, 14, 77

Index

negotiation, 4, 93
non-binding, 16, 39, 63, 70, 72
normal, 32
nuclear, 10, 59, 82
nuclear material, 10, 59
nuclear weapons, 59, 82

O

obligation, 43, 68, 82, 87, 140
obligations, 82
oil, 49, 50, 54, 94, 143
opposition, 70
Organization of American States, 12, 75

P

paramilitary, 44, 74, 78, 141
parents, 150
patriotism, 70, 146
peacekeeping, x, 2, 3, 4, 5, 6, 14, 15, 17, 21,
    45, 46, 53, 61, 65, 68, 69, 70, 74, 76, 77,
    78, 90, 92, 98, 100, 104, 107, 109, 110,
    111, 112, 113, 114, 117, 118, 121, 122
peacekeeping forces, 4, 15, 78
perception, 36
periodic, 12, 25, 79, 84, 108, 139
permit, 5, 12, 23, 29, 35, 112, 129
persuasion, 145
pilots, 10, 59, 123
planning, 107
platforms, 94
play, 150
population, 7, 10, 58, 72, 106
post-Cold War, ix, xi, 27
posture, 152
powers, ix, x, xii, 1, 2, 3, 6, 10, 11, 24, 28,
    29, 30, 36, 37, 46, 52, 56, 60, 64, 68,
    123, 124, 135, 138, 139, 140, 142, 143,
    146, 149, 150, 151, 152, 153
predicate, 85, 142
prejudice, 133
president, 11, 22
press, 44, 57, 93

pressure, 13, 76
printing, 17, 127, 128
private, 102, 103, 104
private citizens, 103
professionalism, 146
property, vi, 17, 19, 20, 58, 118, 121
protection, 16, 50, 63, 64, 70, 93
public, ix, 47, 52, 78, 82, 108
public opinion, 47, 52

Q

quarantine, 32

R

radar, 10, 12, 59
range, xi, 26, 28, 65, 84
reasoning, 38, 148, 149
rebel, 93
reconcile, 71
reconstruction, 62
refuge, 102
refugees, 91, 103
regional, 62, 71, 101, 102, 104, 106, 110,
    111, 113, 114, 115
regular, 9, 35, 71, 129
repair, 32, 125
repatriation, 78
repression, 7, 10, 58, 72, 106
residential, vii, xii, 1, 71, 138
resources, 70, 79, 141
responsibilities, 33, 45, 46, 82, 125
retaliation, 66
ripeness, xii, 138, 139, 152
risk, 32, 40, 144
risks, 14, 77, 148
rotations, 109

S

Saddam Hussein, 54, 82, 133, 150
safety, 33, 37, 70, 102
sanctions, 6, 11, 13, 54, 55, 65, 75, 76, 132

162 Index

school, 78
search, 11, 107
secret, 36
Secretary of Defense, 50, 68, 69, 132
Secretary of State, 5, 41, 49, 65, 66, 68, 132, 135, 147
Secretary-General, 61
seizure, xi, 28, 58, 153
self-government, 108, 111, 112, 113
Senate Foreign Relations Committee, 34, 35, 41, 43, 51, 54, 63, 68
sensitivity, 148
separation, 142, 146, 153
separation of powers, 142, 146, 153
series, 43, 48, 59, 67, 100
shipping, 50, 55
signals, 40, 147
sine, 126
sites, 11, 12
SOC, 107
sovereignty, 93
speed, 86
sponsor, 24, 39
sporadic, 16, 62, 149
stability, 98, 116
stabilization, 19, 20, 120, 121
standards, 45, 140, 142, 148, 153
State Department, 24, 42, 63, 76, 93, 131, 134
statutes, 38, 141, 149
statutory, x, 2, 3, 16, 25, 30, 35, 37, 38, 45, 53, 55, 57, 58, 62, 80, 82, 84, 85, 97, 124, 126, 129, 131, 136, 139, 146, 148, 149, 152
strategies, 87
strength, 32, 51, 58, 62, 114
strikes, 7, 8, 48, 62, 66, 67, 72, 94, 100, 106, 146, 147
suffering, 91
suicide, 46
summer, 12, 51, 74, 82, 104, 108
supplemental, 8, 73, 106, 146
supply, 32, 65, 90, 125, 132
Supreme Court, 9, 24, 34, 38, 43, 74, 75, 130, 142, 146, 147, 149, 151, 153

surprise, 41
surveillance, 93

T

tankers, 49, 143
targets, 10, 12, 44, 59, 61, 68, 94, 96, 101, 123
task force, 10, 59, 106
teeth, 23, 33, 39
tension, 90
territorial, 110, 117
territory, 4, 6, 32, 54, 64, 69, 81, 92, 112, 125, 126, 136
terrorism, xi, 17, 18, 19, 20, 25, 28, 48, 49, 80, 81, 84, 85, 112, 113, 116, 117, 118, 119, 120, 121, 135
terrorist, x, 2, 24, 48, 80, 81, 94, 105, 106, 112, 114, 115, 116, 117, 118, 119, 120, 121, 122
terrorist acts, 48, 81, 112
terrorist attack, x, 2, 24, 80, 81, 112
terrorist organization, 105
terrorists, 3, 19, 20, 21, 79, 81, 83, 112, 115, 117, 120, 121, 122
terrorists attacks, 81
testimony, 68
threat, 14, 19, 20, 25, 26, 49, 59, 66, 77, 80, 81, 82, 83, 84, 85, 97, 102, 112, 120, 129, 154
threatening, 44, 49, 61, 67, 100
threats, 12, 48, 83, 103, 105
threshold, 139
timetable, 82
title, 30
traffic, 13, 76
training, 32, 42, 43, 71, 114, 123, 125, 135
transactions, 13, 76
transition, 62, 107
transport, 91, 122, 123
transportation, 107
treaties, 37, 39, 51, 97, 129
trial, 140, 141, 146, 150
triggers, xi, 28, 31

U

undeclared war, 3, 132
urban areas, 110, 111, 113

V

validity, 38
vehicles, 5, 44
vessels, 40, 48, 76, 91, 94, 95, 99, 110, 149, 153
victims, 64
violence, 7, 14, 62, 72, 77, 97, 106
voice, 29, 83, 146

W

war crimes, 108
war on terror, 3, 17, 18, 19, 20, 21, 118, 119, 120, 121, 122
warfare, 42
weapons, 12, 59, 67, 82, 83, 99, 123, 143
weapons of mass destruction, 82, 83, 123
well-being, 70
wells, 78
wisdom, ix, 1, 58, 144
withdrawal, xii, 8, 15, 23, 36, 38, 39, 40, 45, 46, 48, 54, 56, 63, 73, 74, 78, 82, 87, 88, 89, 91, 92, 100, 102, 103, 138, 148
women, 70
workers, 123
writing, 125, 126